Cambridge Elements ≡

Elements in the Philosophy of Biology
edited by
Grant Ramsey
KU Leuven
Michael Ruse
Florida State University

EXPLANATION IN BIOLOGY

Lauren N. Ross
University of California, Irvine

CAMBRIDGE
UNIVERSITY PRESS

Shaftesbury Road, Cambridge CB2 8EA, United Kingdom

One Liberty Plaza, 20th Floor, New York, NY 10006, USA

477 Williamstown Road, Port Melbourne, VIC 3207, Australia

314–321, 3rd Floor, Plot 3, Splendor Forum, Jasola District Centre, New Delhi – 110025, India

103 Penang Road, #05–06/07, Visioncrest Commercial, Singapore 238467

Cambridge University Press is part of Cambridge University Press & Assessment, a department of the University of Cambridge.

We share the University's mission to contribute to society through the pursuit of education, learning and research at the highest international levels of excellence.

www.cambridge.org
Information on this title: www.cambridge.org/9781009509657

DOI: 10.1017/9781009300940

First published 2024

A catalogue record for this publication is available from the British Library

ISBN 978-1-009-50965-7 Hardback
ISBN 978-1-009-30093-3 Paperback
ISSN 2515-1126 (online)
ISSN 2515-1118 (print)

Explanation in Biology

Elements in the Philosophy of Biology

DOI: 10.1017/9781009300940
First published online: December 2024

Lauren N. Ross
University of California, Irvine

Author for correspondence: Lauren N. Ross, rossl@uci.edu

Abstract: This Element examines philosophical accounts of scientific explanation, particularly those that apply to biology and the life sciences. Two main categories of scientific explanation are examined in detail – causal explanations and non-causal explanations. The first section of this Element provides a brief history and some basics on philosophical accounts of scientific explanation. Section 2 covers causal explanation, first by discussing foundational topics in the area, such as defining causation, causal selection, and reductive explanation. This is followed by an examination of distinct types of causal explanation, including those that appeal to mechanisms, pathways, and cascades. The third section covers non-causal, mathematical explanations, which have received significant attention in philosophy of biology and the life sciences. Three main types of non-causal, mathematical explanation are discussed: topological and constraint-based explanation, optimality and efficiency explanations, and minimal model explanations. This title is also available as Open Access on Cambridge Core.

Keywords: scientific explanation, explanation in biology, causal explanation, mathematical explanation, mechanistic explanation

ISBNs: 9781009509657 (HB), 9781009300933 (PB), 9781009300940 (OC)
ISSNs: 2515-1126 (online), 2515-1118 (print)

Contents

1 Scientific Explanation: Introduction

This Element examines scientific explanations in biology and the life sciences. Explanations are viewed as a "primary" objective of science – they offer deep understanding and knowledge of the world, as opposed to mere descriptions, classifications, and predictions (Hempel 1991, 299). Classically, scientific explanations are viewed as answers to "why-questions" that concern some natural phenomenon of interest (Nagel 1961; Hempel 1965; Bromberger 1966). These include questions such as: Why is the sky blue? Why do cicadas have prime-number year life cycles? Why is this individual sick while others are not? These questions sometimes suggest that an outcome is surprising in a manner that calls out for explanation. An explanation reduces this surprise, showing why the outcome was inevitable and "to be expected" (Hempel 1965, 336). Various accounts of scientific explanation have been proposed in the philosophical literature to capture what distinguishes scientific explanation from other important projects in science. This Element focuses on two main accounts that have received significant attention – causal and non-causal forms of explanation.

1.1 A Brief History

The philosophical literature on scientific explanation has experienced notable shifts since foundational work in the late 1940s, with the rise and fall of different accounts of explanation (Woodward and Ross 2021). A helpful starting point is the influential deductive-nomological (DN) model, articulated by Hempel and Oppenheim in a "first wave" of recent philosophical work on explanation (Hempel and Oppenheim 1948; Baker 2012, 243).[1] This model suggests that scientific explanations are deductive arguments, in which (1) initial conditions and (2) laws of nature are used to (3) deduce and "explain" a target of interest (Hempel and Oppenheim 1948).[2] In order to see the structure of the DN account, consider a mercury thermometer that is placed in boiling water (Hempel 1965). When this thermometer is placed in boiling water, why does the mercury column first dip down in the glass thermometer case and then quickly rise? The explanation for this involves the initial expansion of the glass thermometer casing, which increases its inner volume such that the mercury

---

[1] While the topic of explanation has received significant attention in philosophy, the DN model is often viewed as a helpful starting point for more recent work on the topic.

[2] Attempts to frame explanation in terms of deduction are present as far back as the 4th century BC with Aristotle's explanatory syllogisms (Clatterbaugh 1999).

$$
\begin{array}{l}
\left.\begin{array}{l}
C_1,\ C_2,...,\ C_k \\[2mm]
L_1,\ L_2,...,\ L_k
\end{array}\right\} \quad \text{Explanans}
\end{array}
$$

Deductive-
Nomological
Model

————————————————————————

E　　　　　　　　　Explanandum

Figure 1 The Deductive-nomological model of scientific explanation, rewritten from (Hempel 1965, 336). In this model, the initial conditions are represented by $C_1, C_2, \ldots, C_k$, while the general laws are $L_1, L_2 \ldots, L_k$. The initial conditions and general laws make up the explanans (what does the explanatory work), which deductively lead to the explanandum (or outcome to be explained).

level drops. However, once the temperature reaches the mercury inside, its level rises as mercury has a larger coefficient of expansion than glass. According to Hempel, this explanation is provided by antecedent conditions and general laws (Hempel 1965). The antecedent conditions include the constituents of the thermometer (the glass casing surrounding the mercury) and the fact that the thermometer was placed in boiling water. The general laws include laws about the thermic expansion of glass and mercury and the thermic conductivity of the glass. In this manner, the antecedent conditions and general laws are said to explain and "entail the consequence" that the mercury will drop and rise. On this account, the explanatory target is a "logical consequence" of the relevant antecedent conditions and general laws, with a structure shown in Figure 1.

While the DN model has its strengths, it also suffers from significant problems. First, this model fails to accommodate explanations in sciences that often lack strict, universal laws of nature, such as biology and the life sciences. Genes and environmental factors are cited in explaining traits in organisms, but these explanations rarely (if ever) appeal to general laws from which these traits deductively follow. A second problem is that the DN model fails to capture the directionality of explanation. This is seen in the well-known "flagpole problem," in which a flagpole's height, the sun's location, and laws of optics explain the length of the flagpole's shadow (Hempel 1962; Bromberger 1992).[3] The issue for the DN model is that it incorrectly counts the reverse direction as also explanatory – it implies that the shadow's length (with the sun's location and same general laws) explains the flagpole's height, as this also meets the DN criteria. These and other limitations began to receive attention in the 1960s, which led to increased interest in alternative models of scientific explanation (Woodward and Ross 2021).

————————————————————————

[3] This example first appears in Hempel's work as he recalls a challenge that Bromberger presented to him (Hempel 1962; Bromberger 1992). Many discussions of the flagpole problem cite Bromberger (1966), which lacks discussion of this case (but contains a related Empire State Building example).

One celebrated solution to these problems was found in accounts of causal explanation. On accounts of causal explanation, an outcome is explained by citing the causes that produce it, as causes explain their effects. This solves directionality because causation is asymmetric and contains a clear direction, from cause to effect. This allows one to count the first flagpole scenario as the true explanation, because the explanatory direction is captured by causality – the sun's rays cause, and thus explain, the shadow and not vice versa (Salmon 1989). Another advantage is that the causal framework accommodates explanations in sciences that lack strict laws of nature. These explanations only require causal regularities, which should hold in some set of conditions but need not hold universally. If gene X causes brown coat color in guinea pigs in some background conditions, this explains the trait even if such a regularity does not hold for other animals or in other conditions.

For these and other reasons, causal accounts superseded the DN model as the new reigning view of scientific explanation. This change was supported by increased attention to examples of explanation outside of the physical sciences – such as biology, neuroscience, ecology, and sociology – which were better captured with causal frameworks than the DN model. This encouraged a growing literature on causal explanation and work examining various definitions of causality.[4] This literature would explore a multitude of topics such as causal selection, absence causation, explanatory reduction, causal complexity, causal pluralism, and mechanistic explanation. In this work, causal selection has to do with how to "select" the most explanatory causes (Lewis 1986; Waters 2007; Ross 2018), absence causation concerns whether absences are genuinely causal or not (Beebee 2004), and explanatory reduction pertains to whether lower-level causes are more explanatory than higher-level causes (Sober 1999; Bickle 2006). Causal complexity can refer to situations in which causes are numerous, where causes are related in intricate ways, and where causes are difficult to identify in the world (Wimsatt 1972; Lewis 1986; Mitchell 2009; Ross 2023b). Causal pluralism refers to different projects, including views that there are different legitimate definitions of causation, that there are distinct methods for identifying causality, and that there are different types of causal explanation in science (Cartwright 2004; Hitchcock 2007; Godfrey-Smith 2013). Other work has examined causal mechanisms and mechanistic explanation, in which outcomes are explained by citing the causal mechanisms that produce them. The mechanistic research program has become

---

[4] Examples of different definitions of causation include definitions in terms of regularities (Mackie 1965), connected processes (Salmon 1984), probabilistic relationships (Cartwright 1979; Skyrms 1980), and counterfactuals (Lewis 1986; Woodward 2003).

a mainstream philosophical account of explanatory practice in the life sciences (Machamer et al. 2000; Bechtel and Richardson 2010; Glennan 2017) and what some consider the "dominant view of explanation in the philosophy of science" (Kaplan and Craver 2011). Some work in this area implicitly assumes that all scientific explanations are causal, while other projects directly acknowledge support of this view (Skow 2014).

While the philosophical literature experienced an increase in fruitful work on causation, the view that all scientific explanations are causal would be short-lived. An appreciation for other, non-causal forms of explanation has been supported by examples from many scientific domains. The life sciences have played a central role in these debates as many purported examples of non-causal explanation come from biology, neuroscience, ecology, and so on. Examples of these non-causal explanations include explanations of robust and fragile ecosystems (Huneman 2010), of neural coding and firing behaviors (Ross 2015; Chirimuuta 2018), of the prime number life cycle of cicadas (Baker 2005; Batterman 2010), the hexagonal-shaped honeycombs of bees (Lyon and Colyvan 2008; Lange 2013), and why animal size is limited by the square-cube law (Ross 2023c). In these examples, it is suggested that an important part of the explanatory power comes from mathematics, which is not the case in causal explanations. There are extensive, ongoing debates about how exactly these non-causal, mathematical explanations work – what their features, details, and nature are. As these debates continue, a growing consensus in the field views non-causal, mathematical explanations as legitimate and accepts that scientific explanation is far more diverse than earlier work assumed. While earlier theories of scientific explanation searched for the single, universal account that captures all examples of scientific explanation,[5] more recent work views explanation as a diverse enterprise (Woodward 2019; Woodward and Ross 2021). This brings us to a relatively new position in the field – an appreciation for various types of scientific explanation, without expecting that they all fit a single model, but still requiring that they specify rigorous standards for what counts as explanatory.

This Element focuses on two main categories of scientific explanation – causal and non-causal explanation. These categories of explanation are examined in the context of biology and the life sciences. The discussion of causal explanation (Section 2) will consider foundational topics in this area and three main types of causal explanation – these include explanations that appeal

---

[5] As evidence of this, consider Nagel's claim that the DN model is the "paradigm for any 'genuine' explanation, and has often been adopted as the ideal form to which all efforts at explanation should strive" (Nagel 1961, 21).

to mechanisms, pathways, and cascades (Ross 2021a, In Press). In providing an analysis of non-causal explanation (Section 3), three main classes of non-causal, mathematical explanation will be considered, including topological and constraint-based explanations, optimality and efficiency explanations, and minimal model explanations (Batterman 2001; Baker 2005; Lange 2018). This work will examine similarities and differences across these explanatory patterns – their shared structural features, different guiding principles, and paradigmatic examples of each type. This work balances an appreciation for distinct explanatory patterns, with the view that explanations should meet rigorous standards.

While this work focuses on causal and non-causal explanation, other categories of scientific explanation have been studied. Examples of these other accounts include unificationist explanations (Friedman 1974; Kitcher 1989), narrative and historical explanations (Roth 1988), functional explanations (Wright 1976), and structural explanations (Garfinkel 1981), among others. While causal and non-causal explanation have received significant attention in recent work, questions remain about how they both relate to the other explanation classes mentioned earlier.

This Element is organized in the following manner. The next subsection (1.2) introduces the basics of scientific explanation that will help in understanding the distinct accounts of explanation to come. The second section (2) examines topics in causal explanation including various foundational questions and forms of causal explanation, including mechanism, pathway, and cascade explanations. The third section will discuss types of non-causal, mathematical explanation, including topological and constraint-based explanation, optimality and efficiency explanations, and minimal model explanations. The fourth section will provide concluding remarks on the diversity of scientific explanation in biology and the life sciences.

1.2 The Basics of Explanation

Scientific explanations often involve three main components – the explanandum, explanans, and dependency relation, shown in Figure 2. The *explanandum* is the explanatory target or phenomenon to be explained. The *explanans* is what does the explanatory "work" or provides the explanation. A final component is the *dependency relation* between the explanandum and explanans, which captures how they are related to each other. These elements are found in most explanations, but their features vary across different types of explanation (as will be discussed more soon). Many accounts of scientific explanation elaborate on versions of this three-part model in order to capture the standards

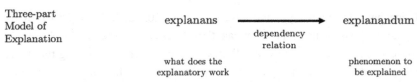

Figure 2 The three-part model of scientific explanation contains: the explanandum (phenomenon to be explained), the explanans (what does the explanatory work), and the dependency relation that connects both. Most philosophical accounts of scientific explanation fit this three-part model, but they differ with respect to what counts as the explanans and how to understand the dependency relation.

that scientific explanations need to meet (Reutlinger 2016; Jansson and Saatsi 2017; Woodward 2019). Identifying these standards is important because it would allow us to distinguish genuine explanations from non-explanations and to determine when explanations are better or worse. The notion of explanation that is examined in this work does not include all broader uses of "explanation" in everyday life, such as explaining the meaning of an expression, how to bake a cake, or why a decision was made (which can involve a detailed description or justification) (Woodward 2003, 4). Instead, it focuses on explanations of natural phenomena, often why they have occurred or why they have particular features.

Discussions of scientific explanation frequently start with the explanatory target. A scientific explanation cannot be provided until the explanatory target is sufficiently clear.[6] In the philosophical literature, the explanatory target is presented as an outcome that scientists are interested in, that they "stumble across by accident" and find surprising, and that calls out for explanation (Hempel 1965; Baker 2005). The target of interest is couched in terms of a why-question, which frames the inquiry and ensuing explanatory quest.

Providing an explanation requires precisely specifying the explanatory target. This precision involves identifying the contrastive focus of interest and meaning of terms in the why-question. Consider the explanatory why-question: "Why does guinea pig A have spotted-coloring on its trunk?" Without further

---

[6] Of course, there may be other ways that scientists start the explanatory process besides first specifying the explanandum of interest. For example, they may be interested in a particular gene and what it explains, controls, and predicts, as in the case of reverse genetics. This involves discovery of the explanatory target after specifying a potential explanans of interest. In this case, we still cannot provide an explanation until the explanandum is specified, but we "discover" the explanandum through an initial interest in a potential explanans. This is related to Rheinberger's idea of "epistemic things," which involve how new "objects come into existence and are shaped in the empirical sciences" (Rheinberger 1997). This also relates to Woodward and Bogen's discussion of the "phenomena" that scientists seek to explain and predict (and how these differ from data, measurements, etc.) (Bogen and Woodward 1988).

clarification, this question is ambiguous and does not sufficiently specify the explanatory target. For example, this question might be asking why guinea pig A has *spotted*-coloring on its trunk versus *solid* coloring; or why guinea pig A has spotted-coloring on its *trunk* as opposed to its *legs*; or why *guinea pig A* has this spotted-coloring as opposed to *guinea pig B*. Each of these contrasts refers to a different explanatory why-question that may have different answers. Specifying the explanatory target with precision is essential for ensuring that scientists are discussing the same explanatory question and not talking past each other. Clarity here helps avoid situations in which scientists mistakenly compare explanations without realizing that the explanations have different targets of interest and, thus, aim to explain different things. This is especially important because natural phenomena can be represented in different ways and have distinct features, which emphasize different contrasts that we might want to explain.

Designating a clear explanatory target also requires defining relevant terms in the explanatory why-question and explanandum. If scientists aim to explain a phenomenon that lacks clear characterization, is ill-defined, or invokes multiple definitions, there are likely to be challenges in providing an explanation. Consider the question, "Why do human beings have lungs?" which we might seek an answer to. As Nagel states, this "question as it stands is ambiguous" because it can be interpreted in distinct ways (Nagel 1961, 19). The principle outlined here is that, if it is not clear what we want to explain, then we are not equipped to provide or assess an explanation. The explanatory target can change through scientific work, but if explanatory potential is to be assessed then some target must be fixed and specified. As a further example, if "consciousness" is defined in myriad or ambiguous ways, then determining how to explain consciousness and whether it has been explained are likely to be contentious and unsettled. If there is little agreement on how to characterize Y, there will likely be little agreement on whether some account explains Y or not.[7] In short, providing an explanation requires that one is very clear about the phenomenon to be explained.

A second main component of scientific explanations is the *explanans* or what does the explanatory work. This is associated with the "answer" that is provided to the explanatory why-question. If we want to explain why guinea pig A's trunk is spotted as opposed to solid-colored, we might appeal to a gene that is responsible for this phenotype. Perhaps other phenotypes (behaviors, disease states, etc.) are caused by environmental factors, such as stress, temperature,

---

[7] In fact, even if there appears to be agreement, we should be skeptical, as the differing meanings of Y can easily produce cross-talk.

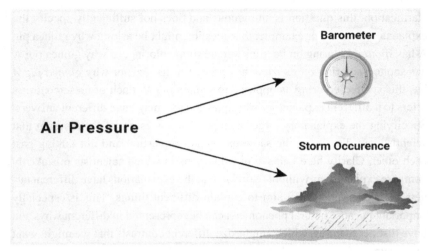

Figure 3 Air pressure is a common cause of both the barometer reading and storm occurrence – air pressure causes and explains both of these outcomes. While the barometer reading accurately predicts (and is correlated with) the storm, it does not cause or explain it.

and contagions. Factors that are cited in explaining the outcome are said to have "explanatory power" with respect to the target of interest. It is common to view these explanatory factors as "difference-makers" for the target of interest, such that changes in the explanans "make a difference" to the states of the explanandum. Relatedly, the explanandum is said to "depend" on the explanatory factors specified in the explanans.

Most philosophical work on scientific explanation is focused on the explanans and criteria that it needs to meet to ensure that a legitimate explanation is provided. Explanations provide deep understanding in a way that is distinct from other scientific projects such as mere description, prediction, and classification. While it is important to describe, predict, and classify distinct guinea pig coat coloring patterns, these are different tasks than explaining why one of these colorings is produced. Accounts of scientific explanation should exclude cases in which a purported explanans simply redescribes or predicts the explanandum. A classic example of the latter is a common cause scenario, shown in Figure 3, in which (A) air pressure causes two distinct outcomes, namely, (1) changes to a barometer reading and (2) changes in storm occurrence (Woodward 2003, 14–15). Notice that the (1) barometer accurately predicts (2) storm occurrence, but we would not say that it explains this outcome. The correlation between (1) and (2) allows this relationship to be useful and reliable, but we are more likely to view both (1) and (2) as caused and explained by the (A) air pressure. This type of example has led to claims that explanatory factors need to do more than simply predict outcomes or make them more probable. Accounts of scientific explanation aim to specify exactly what standards the explanans and explanatory factors need to meet, to ensure that a genuine scientific explanation has been provided.

The third feature of scientific explanations is the dependency relation that connects the explanans and explanandum. It has been suggested that many diverse forms of scientific explanation share this dependency relation feature – that they involve some specification of how the explanandum is dependent on factors in the explanans (Woodward 2003; Reutlinger 2016; Jansson and Saatsi 2017). In some cases, this dependency relation helps distinguish types of explanations, including causal explanations from non-causal, mathematical explanations (Woodward 2019). For causal explanations, this dependency relation is causal as the factors in the explanans and explanandum are connected causally. Alternatively, for some accounts of non-causal explanation, the dependency relation is said to be mathematical and non-empirical in character (Woodward 2019). While causal dependencies are revealed through an empirical, *a posteriori* study of the natural world, mathematical dependencies are identified through mathematical and *a priori* considerations. This difference between causal and mathematical dependencies bears similarity to Hume's distinction between "matters of fact" and "relations of ideas," referred to as "Hume's fork" (Hume 1985). While "matters of fact" are a type of knowledge revealed by experiences of the world, "relations of ideas" are "discoverable independently of experience" as they are logical and mathematical propositions, that are true by definition and known through reason alone (Morris and Brown 2019). Other unique features of these mathematical dependencies are that they can exhibit a stronger form of necessity than standard causal relations (Lange 2018) and they can contain other types of non-causal information (Chirimuuta 2018). This is discussed in more detail in Section 3, which covers different types of non-causal, mathematical explanation.

The focus of this work will be to identify the standards and "formal pattern" of explanation in biology and the life sciences (Nagel 1961). This work aims to strike a balance between capturing standards that scientific explanations should meet, while appreciating that there are different patterns of explanatory practice. Accounts of scientific explanation should capture actual scientific work, but they should also rule out non-explanations. Scientific explanation is not an "anything goes" type of project – correct explanations guide medical treatments, public policy interventions, regulations on our environmental impact, and accounts of how to control and change outcomes in the world. An important role of philosophy involves clarifying the features, characteristics, and structure of scientific explanations and how they give us a principled understanding of the natural world.

2 Causal Explanation

Accounts of causation and causal explanation have received attention in the philosophical literature for over two millennia (Hume 1985; Mill 1874; Aristotle 1970). In the late twentieth century, interest in causal explanation began to increase when it was appreciated that accounts of causal explanation could handle problems faced by the popular deductive-nomological (DN) model of explanation. Since then, there has been significant interest in the features, standards, and types of causal explanation in science. Literature in this area has examined foundational topics, such as defining causation, causal selection, the implications of reduction for scientific explanation, and distinct types of causal explanation, including mechanistic forms and other alternatives. This section provides an overview of these topics.

2.1 Foundational Questions

In the context of causal explanation in biology and the life sciences, three foundational topics include defining causation, causal selection, and reductive explanation. With respect to the first, accounts of causal explanation require defining causation, which involves specifying the characteristic or hallmark features of causality. Once these features are specified, they can be used to distinguish true, genuine causal relationships from everything else, including non-causal relationships and mere correlations. The ability to define causality and reliably make these distinctions is very useful and it has occupied significant attention in philosophy and in science. As causal explanations cite causal factors, a definition of causality is required to identify which factors, relationships, and systems are legitimately causal and capable of providing these explanations. While many different definitions of causation have received attention, four of the most commonly discussed include regularity accounts (Hume 1985; Mackie 1965), connected process accounts (Salmon 1984; Dowe 2018), probabilistic accounts (Suppes 1970; Cartwright 1979), and interventionist accounts (Woodward 2003).[8]

---

[8] Regularity accounts understand causation in terms of regularities or the "constant conjunction" of cause and effect (Hume 1985). Connected process accounts view causal relationships as ones that are capable of transmitting some mark or conserved quantity from cause to effect (Dowe 2018). Probabilistic accounts view causal relationships as captured statistically, often such that causes are factors that increase the probability of their effects (Hitchcock 2018).

While all of these accounts of causation have proponents, one of the most influential and widely used accounts of causation is Woodward's interventionist framework (Woodward 2003).[9] This account is motivated by causal reasoning in scientific contexts, empirical studies of human cognition, and formal methods of causal analysis (Woodward 2021). On the interventionist account of causation, the relata of causal relationships are variables (X, Y, Z, etc.), which represent properties of interest, such as phenotypes, genes, and environmental factors. These variables take on different values (0, 1, 2, etc.) that represent the states of these properties, such as coat color that is brown, gray, and black, or a gene variant that is present or absent. On the interventionist account of causation, to say that X is a cause of Y means that if X were intervened upon and changed, in background conditions B, this would lead to changes in Y. For example, to say that gene G causes a guinea pig's coat to be brown, as opposed to gray or black, means that changes to this gene G (in early development) would have produced a different coat color. In this manner, causes are factors with "control" over their effects, as manipulating them would produce changes to the effect of interest.

This helps reveal the connection between causation and causal explanation. Explaining why, for example, a guinea pig has coat color that is brown, as opposed to other colors, requires citing the cause or causes that "make-a-difference-to" this outcome (Woodward 2003; Waters 2007). In this case, it involves citing a genetic cause because if the genetic cause had been different, in the same set of background conditions, an alternative coat color would have been produced. This reveals the importance of a contrastive focus in specifying an explanatory target and how explanatorily relevant causes should relate to this target. If an environmental factor (such as changes in temperature) met these criteria, then the environmental factor would be viewed as the cause or main cause of coat color. However, true background conditions – such as the presence of oxygen, diet, and so on – should be excluded as main causes and explanations of this phenotype. While background conditions are present and supportive, they are not causally responsible for this phenotype because manipulating them does not control whether the phenotype is in one state or another. If oxygen were manipulated (from present to absent) this would control

---

Finally, interventionist accounts understand causation in terms of interventionist counterfactuals – causes are factors that when intervened upon and changed, produce changes in their effects (Woodward 2003).

[9] For example, Gopnik states that Woodward's interventionist account of causation has "revolutionized the philosophical discussion of causation" (Gopnik 2021). Additionally, Ismael claims that Woodward's book *Making Things Happen* (2003) – in which he details his interventionist account of causation and causal explanation – is arguably "the most important philosophical book about causation to appear in decades" (Ismael 2021).

whether the guinea pig is alive or dead, but this is not the contrastive focus of interest. We are interested in what explains one coat color versus other colors in a *living* guinea pig. When background conditions are required for life, they are necessary conditions for phenotypes to manifest, which prevents them from explaining, causing and controlling the presence of one phenotype versus another. This is why many background conditions do not explain the outcome of interest (even if they seem relevant to it) – they are not explanatory if they do not "make a difference" to the contrastive focus in question.

The interventionist account does not require that causes are actually manipulable with current technology or according to ethical standards. Interventionism just requires that we can consider *hypothetical* manipulations, which involve what would happen if the intervention were to occur (Woodward 2016). This is consistent with causal reasoning in scientific and everyday life contexts, in which we accept causal claims even when we cannot perform interventions on the relevant causal factor(s). Examples of legitimate causes that we cannot intervene on include: historical or past causes ("yesterday the medicine cured my headache"), causes that are not manipulable with current technology ("the location of the moon causes the tides to ebb and flow"), and causes that we cannot manipulate for ethical reasons ("the patient's genes have caused their disease"). The interventionist account includes these as genuine causes because they meet the hypothetical manipulation requirement – in all of these cases, we can consider hypothetical manipulations of the cause, and our evidence and theory supports the claim that this hypothetical manipulation would change the effect of interest.[10] If a purported causal claim cannot be associated with a hypothetical manipulation – perhaps because the suggested changes to the candidate cause are inconsistent with scientific theory or because the purported causes and effects are not sufficiently defined (as mentioned in subsection 1.2) – then this gives good reason to be skeptical that a causal claim has been provided (Woodward 2003, 2016).

Significant amounts of philosophical work has focused on the question of how to define causality. While interventionism provides one answer to this question, there remains the further topic of how many definitions of causation we need to capture causal relationships in the world. This relates to "causal pluralism," which is associated with different views in the literature (Cartwright 2004; Hitchcock 2007; Godfrey-Smith 2013). Three forms of causal pluralism

---

[10] There are various ways to get information about causation even when intervention experiments cannot be performed. Evidence about interventionist difference-making relationships can be supported by quasi-experiments, instrumental variables, observational methods, natural experiments, and other methods and aspects of biological theory (Shadish et al. 2002; Angrist and Pischke 2009).

to keep distinct are definitional pluralism, methodological pluralism, and (what I call) structural pluralism. Definitional pluralism about causation claims that we need two or more definitions of causation to capture causality in the world. Definitional monism about causation claims that we only need one definition of causation to capture causality in the world. Alternatively, methodological pluralism refers to the number of methods that can identify (or provide evidence of) causality in the world (Shadish et al. 2002; Reiss 2009). A methodological pluralist claims that many methods can be used to identify causal relationships, while a methodological monist claims that only one method can provide this (with a main contender being randomized control trials).[11] A third type of causal pluralism–structural pluralism about causation – captures distinct causes and causal systems that can meet the same definition of causation, but differ with respect to other features. Examples discussed later in this section are mechanisms, pathways, and cascades, which are distinct causal systems (Ross 2021a, In Press). Further examples are differences between causes that are proximal, distal, predisposing, exciting, and organized in different manners (such as linear chains, feedback loops, etc.). While these causal systems can all meet the same definition of causation, they differ with respect to other features. While most scholars accept some type of structural pluralism, versions of structural monism are seen in claims that all causal systems are best understood as "mechanisms" no matter what their differences are (Craver 2007; Levy and Bechtel 2013; Craver and Tabery 2015).[12]

A second foundational topic in the area of causality has to do with causal selection, which refers to selecting or identifying causes that are the most explanatory for an outcome. Consider that the number of causally relevant factors for any target of interest can be seemingly "infinite" (Lewis 1986, 214). For any explanatory target, there appear to be an enormous set of factors far "back" in its causal history (extending back to the Big bang) and far "down" at lower scales (such as fundamental physics). While this list of factors is nearly endless, we do not view all of these causes as equally explanatory for the outcome – only

---

[11] *The Journal of the American Medical Association* (JAMA) prohibits authors from using "causal language" (including "effect" and "efficacy") in their submitted papers unless a "randomized clinical trial" has been conducted that supports the work. As they state, "all other study designs (including meta-analyses of randomized clinical trials), methods and results should be described in terms of association or correlation and should avoid cause-and-effect wording" (JAMA 2023). This strict view is consistent with a methodological monist position about causality.

[12] While these accounts often appreciate different types of mechanisms, they still maintain that all causal systems are of one "type" in a way suggestive of a monist view. The claim is not just that these systems are all causal (which is trivially true as they are causal systems), but that they share some further "mechanism" feature that unifies all causal systems, as opposed to capturing pluralism.

a few are selected as the main, explanatory causal factors. A main question for any account of explanation is how to determine which factors are most explanatory and why. What guidelines or criteria distinguish causal factors that are more explanatory from those that are less explanatory? In philosophy of science, there are longstanding debates about whether a cogent rationale for causal selection exists or if it is hopelessly unprincipled. For example, Mill and Lewis have claimed that causal selection is guided by "capricious" and "invidious" sentiments, respectively (Mill 1874; Lewis 1986). Lewis suggests that when we select the main causes of an outcome, that this is guided merely by our interest in these causes, the fact that we find these causes to be good or bad, or simply because they are causes under our control. These claims suggest that causal selection is guided by arbitrary, subjective, and non-scientific reasons.[13] Such a position is problematic for the view that scientific explanation has a principled nature – if causal explanation and causal selection are guided by principled considerations, these principles and the role they play need to be specified.

In the biological sciences, a central example of causal selection is genetic causation, in which genes are viewed as the main cause for various traits (sickle cell disease, Huntington's disease, etc.). Significant literature has focused on what rationale justifies privileging genes as the main causes for these outcomes. An important tool that can be used to address these questions involves clarifying various "distinctions among causation," which capture objective differences across types of causal factors Woodward (2010, 2021). For example, some causes are more specific, stable, strong, or fast than others – these differences can figure in why some are more or less explanatory for an outcome. It has been suggested that genes are prioritized in scientific explanations, because they are more specific and stable than other causal factors (Waters 2007; Woodward 2010; Weber 2017, 2022). A specific cause (in the sense used in these discussions) is a cause that produces fine-grained control over an outcome – this is seen when specific changes in DNA result in fine-grained changes in the protein product created.[14] This type of specificity can be understood as a cause variable with many values, in which each values corresponds to

---

[13] As Lewis states, "We sometimes single out one among all the causes of some event and call it 'the' cause, as if there were no others. Or we single out a few as the 'causes,' calling the rest mere 'causal factors' or 'causal conditions' . . . I have nothing to say about these principles of invidious discrimination" (Lewis 1986, 558–559).

[14] A second type of causal specificity refers to the number of cause variables for an effect (specificity of cause) and the number of effect variables for a cause (specificity of effect) (Woodward 2010; Ross In Press). In this case specificity refers to "one" cause or effect (not fine-grained control) and non-specific refers to many causes or many effects. An example of non-specificity of effect is pleiotrophy, which refers to a single gene that produces many different effects.

a unique value in the effect variable. (This is similar to a dimmer switch that has fine-grained control over the brightness of a light.) This is contrasted with a non-specific cause, in which binary values of the cause variable control a binary outcome of the effect (as seen in an on/off switch for the on/off of a light bulb). Additionally, a stable cause is a factor that exerts its causal influence across a wide range of changes in background conditions. Consider that various gene mutations are stable in the sense that they cause disease in patients even when there are differences in diet, childhood upbringing, and other environmental factors (Kendler 2005; Woodward 2010). Research in empirical psychology shows that humans view stable causes as more paradigmatically causal than less stable causes, and stable causes clearly have advantages when it comes to understanding and control (Cheng 1997; Lombrozo 2010; Vasilyeva et al. 2018).

Another important causal distinction, especially in the context of causal selection and explanatory causes, is causal strength. The strength of a causal relationship refers to the degree to which a cause increases the probability of its effect or produces a large magnitude of change in its effect.[15,16] A classic example are Mendelian genes, which are frequently described as having causal action that is "deterministic" in the sense that the presence of the gene ensures occurrence of the trait (Kendler 2005). Other causes are said to be "probabilistic" as they increase the probability of their effects, without guaranteeing or determining them (Parascandola and Weed 2001; Kendler 2005).[17] Similar to specificity and stability, causal strength is a feature that comes in degrees, as causes can differ continuously with respect to how probability boosting their causal influence is. Many paradigmatic causes in biology and the life sciences are not only highly stable (according to the aforementioned description), but also rank high in terms of strength. This is seen for Mendelian traits and diseases that fit the monocausal model – most of these cases cite single causes that produce their effects with a high probability and in a wide range of contexts.[18] While stability is similar to the "generalizability" of a causal relationship, strength is similar to scientific discussions of "deterministic" and

---

[15] This notion of causal strength is similar to what Cheng (1997) refers to as causal power. For more on this see: (Cheng 1997; Griffiths and Tenenbaum 2005; Woodward 2021).

[16] This framework differs from definitions of causation in terms of causes increasing the probability of their effects (Suppes 1970; Salmon 1977; Cartwright 1979). On this view, an interventionist account can be used to define causation Woodward (2003), and the strength of a causal relationship is secondary – a sort of extra causal feature.

[17] This feature of strength also relates to debates over genetic determinism, which concerns whether genes alone determine outcomes of interest.

[18] Examples include the pathogenic gene for Huntington's disease (HD) and the lack of dietary vitamin C causing scurvy.

"probabilistic" causes, which concerns whether a cause guarantees its effect or not (or how probability boosting it is for its effect). Factors that are often referred to as "sufficient causes" often rank high in terms of both stability and strength (and notions of sufficient causation can problematically conflate these distinct causal varieties).

Many other distinctions among causation have been studied in recent work. These include whether causes produce their effects in ways that are fast or slow, irreversible or reversible, in ways that transfer material to the effect or not, and in ways that are proportional (Woodward 2010; Ross 2018; Ross and Woodward 2022; Ross 2023a).[19] Research into these and other causal distinctions is a helpful approach, in efforts to capture how main, explanatory causes can (and should be) distinguished from less explanatory causes. The fact that scientific communities often reach consensus on the main causes of outcomes – and that these causes serve specific goals, such as control – supports the view that causal selection in science is often guided by principled considerations, as opposed to ever-changing subjective preferences.

A third foundational topic in the causation literature is explanatory reduction, which refers to how far "down" an explanation should go when citing causal factors (Mayr 1989).[20] These debates commonly reference a "layer cake" picture of the world, in which phenomena differ with respect to the "scale" or "level" they reside on (Batterman 2001; Waters 2009; Potochnik 2021). This view suggests a hierarchical picture in which distinct sciences focus on different scales or levels – the lower levels are studied by physics, the next higher levels by chemistry, and further increasing levels are the focus of biology, psychology, and various social sciences (Wimsatt 1976; Sober 1999).[21] Suppose an explanatory target is specified in the context of biology, such as an organism's phenotype. With respect to this phenotype, are explanations that cite factors from lower biological scales – such as molecular biology – better than explanations that cite factors from higher-scales such as cellular networks, neural circuits, pathways, and system-level topologies? Will the best explanations of these outcomes cite causes from the biological scale or should it ultimately

---

[19] Proportionality refers to causes and effects being on the same "level" or scale of description. For example, suppose a gene variant is known to cause individuals to (i) seek out "sensation-seeking" activities, in general. If one were to claim, instead, that the gene causes individuals to (ii) seek out extreme sports, bungee-jumping, speeding, and sky diving, we could say that (i) is more proportional than (ii), in the sense that (i) contains descriptions of cause and effect that are on the same level of description (Kendler 2005; Woodward 2010).

[20] For helpful work on the features and limits of reduction in biology see: (Bickle 2006; Brigandt 2010; Hüttemann and Love 2011; O'Malley et al. 2014; Kaiser 2015; Barwich 2021).

[21] Scientific fields outside of fundamental physics are sometimes called "the special sciences" or simply, "higher-level" sciences, in this literature (Fodor 1974).

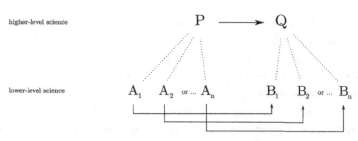

Figure 4 Based on Fodor (1974) and Sober (1999).

include causes from chemistry and physics? Many who argue for explanatory reduction claim that the best explanations – even of biological outcomes – will ultimately cite causal factors from lower-levels (Sober 1999; Strevens 2008; Butterfield 2011).

These questions about explanatory reduction can be illustrated with Sober's discussion of explanations of lung cancer (Sober 1999). In this case, the higher-level causal regularity is "smoking cigarettes causes lung cancer," which is represented by "$P \rightarrow Q$" in Figure 4. In this example, causal variable P "smoking cigarettes" is realized by different lower-level carcinogens, namely, carcinogens $A_1, A_2, \ldots A_n$. Similarly, effect variable Q "lung cancer" is realized by distinct cellular cancer types, namely, $B_1, B_2, \ldots B_n$. A main question with respect to this example is which causal factors best explain the higher-level lung cancer phenotype Q? In particular, are causes at lower or higher levels more explanatory?

Sober claims that lower-level causal details provide objectively superior explanations when compared to higher-level causes. He claims that, while higher-level causal detail might be preferred by some scientists and might give explanatory breadth, this higher-level causal detail never provides an objectively superior explanation compared to lower-level causal details (Sober 1999; Ross 2020). Sober argues for this position with three main points. First, he claims that lower-level causes can always be included in an explanation, without reducing explanatory power, while the same cannot be said for higher-level causes. He suggests that lower-level causal detail is never unexplanatory – it might be more than a scientist wants to hear, but at worst it (simply) "explains too much" (Sober 1999). In other words, just because we "may not want to hear the gory details … does not mean that the details are not explanatory" (Sober 1999, 549). Second, Sober claims that lower-level causes are what do the real "work" in producing the explanatory target of interest and that this justifies their explanatory priority over higher-level causes (Sober 1999, 548). A final point he makes is that lower-level causal detail – such as detail from fundamental physics – has the advantage of providing "causal completeness," which cannot be supplied by higher-level causal detail. As he states, "if singular occurrences can be explained by citing their causes, then the causal completeness of physics ensures that physics has a variety of explanatory completeness that other sciences do not possess" (Sober 1999). In other arguments in the literature, explanatory reduction is supported by views that higher-level detail provides "shallow explanations" compared to "deeper accounts" provided by lower-level causal information (Waters 1990).

In contrast to explanatory reduction, I suggest that a level-agnostic view of causal explanation is more compelling. On a level-agnostic view of causal explanation the most explanatorily relevant causes for an outcome can be at any scale or level (not just at lower-levels). Indeed, in some cases, higher-level causes are more explanatory than lower-level causal details. The guiding principles of this framework are that (i) the level of causal detail that is explanatory depends on the explanatory target of interest and (ii) the explanatorily relevant causes should "make a difference to" and provide control over this explanatory target. In some cases, higher-level causes better meet these standards than lower-level ones – this captures the principled reasons for why the higher-level causes are more explanatory. The pithy way to capture this level-agnostic view is to say—causal explanation is not a game of how low can you go, but what gives you control. In some cases, the causes with control (over the effect) are at higher scales.

The strength of this level-agnostic view of causal explanation can be illustrated with Sober's lung cancer example and discussions of multiple realizability (Putnam 1967; Fodor 1974; Ross 2020). Multiple realizability refers to situations in which some higher-level phenomenon x (such as smoking cigarettes) is multiply realized by distinct lower-level details, $z_1, z_2, \ldots z_n$ (such as distinct carcinogens that vary across cigarette types). In the context of Sober's smoking example, the multiple realization of x relates to a type of causal complexity – called causal heterogeneity – in which distinct causes or combinations of causes $(z_1, z_2, \ldots z_n)$ are all individually sufficient to produce the same effect (y). This is seen in Figure 5 that captures how distinct lower-level carcinogens $(z_1, z_2, \ldots z_n)$ are all able to cause the same higher-level lung cancer outcome (y).

Suppose that our explanatory why-question is: "What is the cause of lung cancer in this population?" If we want to explain this type or population level target y – all cases of lung cancer – there is a problem with appealing to a lower-level carcinogen, such as z_1. The problem is that this lower-level cause z_1 only "makes a difference" to and explains a small fraction of lung cancer cases and we want to explain all of them. Intervening on z_1 does not control

higher-level science

lower-level science

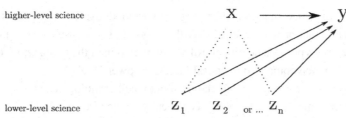

Figure 5 This diagram is based on Fodor (1974) and Sober (1999). The property x is multiply realized by $z_1, z_2, \ldots z_n$, and each of these realizers is a cause of y, making y causally heterogeneous.

or account for all lung cancer outcomes, as the other lung cancer outcomes are produced by other causes ($z_2, z_3 \ldots$). Alternatively, a clear advantage of the higher-level causal factor "smoking cigarettes" (x) is that it does "make a difference to" and provide control over all (or most) instances of this disease. Preventing most or all lung cancer outcomes is possible with smoking cessation, unlike interventions on specific carcinogens, which differ across cigarette types. This is why public health campaigns purposefully target smoking habits (and not individual carcinogens) in their efforts to reduce lung cancer. However, if the explanatory target is a token or single instance of lung cancer, the lower-level carcinogen can easily surpass the higher-level cause in explanatory power. In this case, the lower-level cause "makes-a-difference" to the outcome and provides control over it. An issue with Sober's analysis is that it focuses on the token-outcome explanation, while multiple realizability arguments are concerned with type-level explanatory targets (Ross 2020). As life scientists often want to understand and explain reoccurring, type-level outcomes, the challenge of multiple realizability (and citing lower level-causes) is significant. A central message in this analysis is that the causal factors that are explanatory and the "level" that they reside at can change with the explanatory target of interest.[22]

A main suggestion of this analysis is that different explanatory targets can require different levels of causal detail – there is not a particular level of causal detail that is always privileged or objectively better in providing scientific

---

[22] Can the reductive explanation be saved by citing a disjunctive set of lower-level carcinogens? One problem with this is that it is not clear how to intervene on (or perform a scientific experiment on) a disjunction – as explanatory causes need to meet this feature, this is problematic for viewing a disjunction as causally responsible and explanatory. Second, we also expect explanations to be contained, unified answers to explanatory why-questions – if the response to the why-question involves citing a set of 300 disjunctive properties and it is not clear how they relate to each other, or what they have in common, we are left unsatisfied with the explanation. This large set of disjuncts is also unhelpful in designing targets for control, as they suggest targeting 300 different factors to control the outcome, in contrast to targeting a shared causal process, such as "smoking cigarettes."

explanations. Once an explanatory target is specified, explanatory causes need to be factors that provide control over the target. In some cases, causal factors at higher-levels provide better control and explanation of the explanatory target of interest, when compared to causal factors at lower-levels.

Finally, it is worth addressing claims about whether biology can be – in principle or in some future science – completely reduced to or explained away with fundamental physics. Some challenges for such claims are that they are often guesses or desires about future science, without reflecting actual scientific work. These guesses differ from person to person, and they are difficult to support with evidence or argument. In other cases, such claims are motivated by metaphysical or philosophical assumptions about the nature of the world (perhaps about how all biological phenomena supervene on fundamental physics). The work provided in this Element takes more of a methodological orientation in using science and scientific methods to settle such questions. Attention to actual work in the life sciences encourages skepticism of strongly reductive claims about explanation. Researchers in biology and the life sciences have a strong track record of successfully identifying causes and providing causal explanations. Medical researchers have successfully identified causes of diseases, neuroscientists identify axonal, circuit, and network causes of behavior, and ecologists discover the causes of ecosystem perturbations. That scientists are successful is supported by their use of these causal relationships to change the world – they have eliminated diseases from the planet (such as smallpox), developed effective treatments for neurological conditions (such as epilepsy), and restored ecosystem stability (as in the reintroduction of the gray wolf population to Yellowstone National Park). These successes are not attributable to fundamental physics – they are the fruits of the biological and life sciences. Capturing scientific explanation and scientific successes in biology, neuroscience, and ecology requires appreciating the actual scientific methods, assumptions, and reasoning that are present in these scientific domains.

2.2 Mechanistic Explanation

So far, this discussion has focused on definitions of causation and the rationale behind viewing particular causes as explanatory. Much of this work focuses on single (or a few) main causal factors, but most outcomes in biology and the life sciences are multicausal, as they are the result of many interacting causes (L. N. Ross 2023b). Mechanistic explanations accommodate this multicausal perspective as they cite causal mechanisms – which contain multiple causes – that produce the explanatory target of interest. Accounts of mechanistic explanation have been extremely influential, leading to views that mechanistic explanation is the "dominant view of explanation in the philosophy of science at present" (Kaplan and Craver 2011).

Modern accounts of mechanistic explanation have three main influences. A first influence is the seventeenth-century mechanical philosophy views of Descartes, Newton, Boyle, and others (Henry 2001). This mechanist work opposed vitalist conceptions of living systems, as vitalist conceptions explained natural phenomena by appealing to occult powers, vital forces, and magical properties. Alternatively, the mechanist framework explained living systems with the "mathematical discipline of mechanics," in which systems were divisible into lower-level entities that interact through "contact action" to produce behaviors of the system (Clatterbaugh 1999; Henry 2001). This framework was reductive in appealing to causes at lower-scales and it defined causation in terms of action, physical forces, and matter in motion. This mechanistic perspective relied heavily on the analogy of living systems to machines – both were said to contain lower-level parts that mechanically interact, similar to the levers, pulleys, and pipes in simple machines (Henry 2001). Modern accounts of mechanistic explanation are referred to as "new" mechanist accounts in order to acknowledge their origin in this earlier work, but also to distinguish them from it. These modern accounts retain a focus on mechanisms as constitutive (in containing lower-level parts) and as providing reductive explanations, but they sometimes distance themselves from direct analogy of mechanisms to machines (Craver and Tabery 2015).

A second main influence on new mechanist accounts of explanation is Salmon's "causal mechanical" model of explanation, which relies on a connected process view of causation (Salmon 1984). Connected process accounts of causation maintain that genuine causal processes are capable of transmitting marks through their steps, while non-causal, "pseudo-processes" are incapable of reliably transmitting marks. Examples of causal processes and the marks they transmit are: scuffs on a fly baseball, snow on the roof of a railcar, carved initials on a flying arrow, and chalk marks on a sequence of colliding billiard balls (Reichenbach 1971; Salmon 1984; Woodward 2016). In all of these cases, some physical mark moves through the causal process in question. A shadow that moves alongside an object in motion is a pseudo-process – the shadow is non-causal because it cannot reliably transmit a mark (while the traveling object can). Although there are different conceptions of what counts as a "mark," in much of this work various types of properties have counted, such as "constituent material, bonding forces . . . geometrical shape" (Dowe 2018) and "momentum, energy, or electric charge" (Salmon 1997). A significant feature of Salmon's causal mechanical model is his suggestion that the causal structure of the world is mechanistic. He views explanation as a project of fitting an explanandum into the "causal nexus" of the world, and this causal nexus is exclusively mechanistic. This supports an expansive notion of mechanism as mechanism captures the entire causal structure of the world. While modern accounts of mechanistic explanation seldom rely on Salmon's connected process account of causation, they share many other features. For example, contemporary accounts of mechanistic explanation adopt Salmon's view that the causal structure of the world is mechanistic, they often view all causal explanations as mechanistic, and they often agree that mechanisms come in constitutive and etiological varieties (Salmon 1984). With respect to defining causation, many mechanistic analyses either rely on an interventionist account or they are silent on what definition of causation should be used to understand their notion of mechanism (Craver 2007; Bechtel and Richardson 2010; Craver and Tabery 2015).[23]

Finally, a third main influence on – and motivation for – mechanistic accounts is the fact that scientists commonly use the mechanism concept in biology and the life sciences. Biologists and life science researchers frequently use the term "mechanism" when they describe causal systems and provide explanations. This is seen in appeals to the mechanisms of gene expression, mechanisms of neuron signal propagation, a drug's mechanism of action, reference to various circuit and network mechanisms of the brain, and so on (Pickrell et al. 2010; Cole et al. 2016; Masse et al. 2019). While scientists commonly appeal to mechanisms in explaining outcomes, philosophers are interested in specifying what type of causal structure mechanism refers to, such that the standards, features, and nature of these explanations can be clarified and understood.

The philosophical literature on mechanisms and mechanistic explanation is vast. There are many different accounts of mechanism and mechanistic explanation and they are applied to various questions in philosophy (Andersen 2014a,b). While there is no consensus on how to understand mechanisms, some common claims emerge in the literature. These include claims about the features of mechanisms, their association with the machine analogy, and claims that they are studied with the investigative strategies of decomposition and localization.

In terms of what causal structures count as mechanisms, a first common claim is that mechanisms are hierarchical, in the sense that they contain lower-level causal parts that interact together to produce a higher-level outcome

---

[23] One exception to this is found in the work of Glennan, in which mechanism is used to provide an account of causation (Glennan 2017).

Explanandum

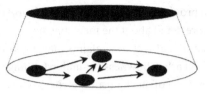

Mechanism

Figure 6 Mechanism. This figure captures the hierarchical feature of mechanisms, in which they are systems with lower-level causes that produce higher-level outcomes of the system. Similar representations are found in Craver (2007) and Craver and Tabery (2015).

of the system.[24] This feature of mechanisms is also referred to as "part-whole," "constitutive," "componential," or as having a "nested character," as these terms capture the difference in level or scale of causal parts to their effect (Craver 2007, 108). This feature is often represented with an illustration similar to the one shown in Figure 6, in which lower-level causal parts all interact to produce a higher-level outcome of the system. Emphasis on this hierarchical feature reveals how these new mechanist accounts are similar to seventeenth-century notions of mechanism and to Salmon's constitutive notion of mechanism. It also shows how the new mechanist framework supports a reductive picture of scientific explanation, in which outcomes are explained by lower-level causes.

Second, it is commonly claimed that mechanisms contain significant amounts of fine-grained detail. In this manner, simple monocausal models (that specify one cause for an effect) do not count as mechanisms and highly sparse network models do not count as mechanisms either. This point is argued by Craver who captures the completeness of mechanism representations on a "continuum" of more or less detail (Craver 2007). On this picture, less-detailed causal representations are mere "sketches" or "schema" that are not yet complete mechanisms. These "incomplete" mechanism representations leave gaps and use filler terms that "veil failures of understanding" or provide an

---

[24] This common notion of mechanism is similar to Salmon's "constitutive" mechanisms, which he distinguishes from "etiological" mechanisms (Salmon 1984). While constitutive mechanisms have lower-level causes in a part-whole system, etiological mechanisms have upstream causes along a linear chain (Salmon 1984). Although Salmon considers both of these causal structures mechanisms, the current mechanism literature focuses almost entirely on the hierarchical, constitutive, and part-whole form of mechanism. In fact, etiological causal systems are more similar to other causal concepts, such as pathways, which many new mechanists distinguish from genuine mechanisms (Craver and Darden 2013). These non-mechanistic causal systems are discussed in the next two subsections.

"illusion of understanding" (Craver and Darden 2013, 113–114). On this view, making "progress" in providing causal explanations involves moving along this continuum to gain more detail about the mechanism (Craver and Darden 2013, 113–114). These points are also seen in claims that sparse causal structures are "incomplete" and reflect a "shallowness" of understanding and that monocausal models are "[t]he sketchiest of mechanism sketches" (Craver and Darden 2013; Glennan 2017).[25] On these accounts, in order for a causal structure to count as a mechanism and to be sufficiently explanatory, it must contain some significant amount of causal detail.

A third common claim about mechanisms is that the causal relationships they contain are described in terms of mechanical interactions, such as force, action, and motion. In a mechanism, it is not enough to say *that* X causes Y – one needs to say *how* X causes Y, often in terms of mechanical interactions and detail. For example, these mechanistic interactions can involve specifying that X splices, activates, triggers, opens or binds to Y.[26] This third feature of mechanisms is related to the second feature in the sense that when you give additional information about how a cause produces its effect you also serve the second feature by providing more detail about the system.

In addition to these three features, mechanisms in the life sciences are often analogized to machines and they are studied with causal investigative strategies that include decomposition and localization (Bechtel and Richardson 2010). With respect to the former, causal structures that scientists refer to as mechanisms are often claimed to be machine-like. Examples from molecular biology include referring to enzymes as "motors," "biological ratchets," and "molecular machines" (Mahadevan and Matsudaira 2000; Endow 2003). The fact that mechanisms in the life sciences are analogized to machines is unsurprising, because many everyday life machines share the three main mechanism features listed earlier.[27] Finally, it is often suggested that mechanisms are studied with the investigative strategies of decomposition and localization (Bechtel and Richardson 2010). These strategies involve fixing an explanatory outcome and then drilling down to identify the lower-level causal parts

---

[25] An example of mechanism that differ from this is found in the work of Levy and Bechtel (2013), in which they argue for abstract causal mechanisms (Levy and Bechtel 2013).

[26] This mechanical interaction feature is related to the new mechanist's focus on verbs in capturing mechanism activities (Machamer et al. 2000) and prior work that focuses on the added causal content of verbs and "thick" causal concepts (Anscombe 1971; Cartwright 2004)

[27] We see this in everyday life machines, such as car engines and watch mechanisms – both contain lower-level parts that produce a higher-level behavior of the system, causal representations of these systems are highly detailed, and descriptions of their causal relationships emphasize force, action, and motion.

that produce this outcome. These strategies are related to the hierarchical organization of mechanisms and the fact that they are defined by and relative to single explanatory targets (Ross 2021a). The explanatory target of interest is what fixes the particular "parts" and circumscribes the bounds of the causal mechanical system.

Mechanistic accounts of explanation have received enormous attention in recent philosophical literature on scientific explanation. Central questions in this literature concern the exact character of mechanistic explanation and its prevalence in biology and the life sciences. With respect to the prevalence of mechanistic explanation, consider two questions that capture different views on this topic:

1. Are all *explanations* in the life sciences mechanistic or is mechanistic explanation one type of *explanation* in this domain?
2. Are all *causal explanations* in the life sciences mechanistic or is mechanistic explanation one type of *causal explanation* in this domain?

In early work, many new mechanists supported an explanatory monist position with respect to (1) and argued that all explanations in biology and the life sciences are mechanistic (Machamer et al. 2000; Craver 2007; Bechtel and Richardson 2010; Kaplan and Craver 2011). On this view "explanations are said to be adequate to the extent, and only to the extent, that they describe the causal mechanisms that maintain, produce, or underlie the phenomenon to be explained" (Kaplan and Craver 2011). These claims were viewed by many as overly bold and "imperialist" in claiming that mechanistic explanation is the exclusive form of explanation in the life sciences (Kaplan 2017). These explanatory monist claims were strongly countered by various discussions of the limits of mechanistic explanation (Weber 2008; Dupré 2013; Woodward 2013; Skillings 2015; Halina 2018; Ross 2021a) and myriad examples of non-causal, mathematical explanations, which explain without appealing exclusively to causal information (Silberstein and Chemero 2013; Batterman and Rice 2014; Ross 2015; Chirimuuta 2018). These non-causal explanation types have been overwhelmingly accepted in the philosophical literature on scientific explanation (and they are discussed more in the next subsection). Many new mechanists have been convinced by positions on non-causal (and, thus, non-mechanistic) explanation and they have revised their views to acknowledge the legitimacy of these explanation types.

However, in revising their views, many new mechanists have adopted a second monist position, captured by the second (2) question earlier. These new mechanists have adopted monism about causal explanation, which claims that all *causal* explanations in the life sciences are mechanistic.[28] The tenability of this position depends on how "mechanism" is defined and understood. Notice that if mechanism is defined narrowly by the three features earlier (constitutive organization, fine-grained detail, and mechanical interactions), or by any particular features, this conflicts with the monist position – this is because there are a great variety of distinct causal structures that are cited in biological and life science explanations, and there is no specific set of features that are shared across all of these causal structures. For example, some explanations cite higher-level causes that produce lower-level outcomes, other explanations appeal to causal systems that are sparse and abstract away from detail (such as topological and network models), and yet other explanations refer to causal systems with linear, causal chain organizations. As these do not share the previously outlined mechanism features, they qualify as non-mechanistic causal systems. These are just three alternative causal structures – many other diverse causal systems exist and are cited in life science explanations. Thus, an important question to ask is, given the variety of causal systems that figure in life science explanations, which of these causal systems count as mechanisms?

While many new mechanist accounts began with specific, narrower conceptions of mechanism (such as the three-feature account earlier), recent accounts have broadened the notion of mechanism to the point of equating it with nearly any type of causal system. This broad notion of mechanism is seen in accounts that refrain from specifying any defining or characteristic features of mechanisms. For example, some of these accounts claim that mechanisms can be highly detailed or not, machine-like or not, reductive or not, driven by push-pull dynamics or not, and so on (Craver and Tabery 2015). Whichever feature it is suggested that some mechanisms have, it is quickly stated that other mechanisms need not have this feature. Similarly, when these new mechanists state what does not count as a mechanism, they tend to only provide examples of non-causal systems (these are obviously not mechanistic because they are not causal). Insofar as helpfully articulating the mechanism concept requires specifying what does and does not count as a mechanism, many of these broad

---

[28] For example, Kaplan and Craver (2011) state that "models in "lower-level" neuroscience, carry explanatory force to the extent, and only to the extent, that they reveal (however dimly) aspects of the causal structure of a mechanism" (Kaplan and Craver 2011, 602). Similarly, Glennan (2017) states "The phenomena that constitute our world are the products of mechanisms: car engines are mechanisms for rotating drive shafts; eyes are mechanisms for transducing light into neural impulses; oxidation is a mechanism that produces rust" (Glennan 2017). This monist claim is also found implicitly in the literature, in the sense that discussions of non-mechanistic explanation focus on identifying explanations that are non-causal as it is often assumed that all causal explanations (and those causal concepts figuring in them) are mechanistic (Kaplan and Craver 2011; Silberstein and Chemero 2013; Chirimuuta 2018).

views have been found to be overly expansive and wanting by many. As Dupré states, "if the concept of a mechanism is to do any work, we must surely have some sense of what isn't a mechanism" (Dupré 2013). I will add that we must also have a sense of what causal systems are not mechanisms; otherwise, the term is only as meaningful as "causal system," despite being advertised as much more.

It is clear that many distinct types of causal systems figure in explanations in biology and the life sciences. The question is whether to view some of these causal systems as mechanisms (narrow mechanism view) or to view all of these causal systems as mechanisms (broad mechanism view).[29] Challenges for the broad mechanism view are that it threatens to over-expand and trivialize the notion of mechanism by equating it with generic notions of "causal system" or "causation." In many scientific and everyday life contexts, mechanism implies much more than "causal system" or "causality" – "mechanism" is often a high-status causal term that communicates knowledge of significant detail and information (Hutchinson 2007; Ankley et al. 2010). Furthermore, if "mechanism" just means "causal system," then accounts of mechanistic explanation are limited in what they add to our understanding of causal explanation in science. Since the fall of the DN model, accounts of causal explanation have received significant attention. These accounts claim that causes explain their effects and they define causation in order to capture how these explanations work. Accounts of mechanistic explanation have entered this scene and their main contribution is that "causal explanations cite mechanisms." However, if "mechanism" is synonymous with "causal system," then these accounts are merely stating that "causal explanations cite causal systems." This is obvious, tautological, and something we already knew – it is implied by the causal explanation framework and it fails to add to our understanding of how these explanations work. Thus, it is worth questioning whether the broad notion of mechanism advances our understanding of explanation in the life sciences and whether it captures the use of mechanism in these domains.

Whether one adopts a narrow or broad notion of mechanism, most agree that accounts of causal explanation should capture the diversity of causal systems that are explanatory. This Element adopts a narrow conception of mechanism – captured by the three features earlier – and examines other types of causal systems and causal explanation in the life sciences. Two other types

---

[29] Scientists also appear to use the term "mechanism" in varying ways. This can lead to challenges when publications and grants are assessed in terms of whether they reveal "mechanistic insights" which is a standard often found in journal publication guidelines and grant calls (Seals 2023; Andersen 2008). For more on this in the context of neuroscience see: Ross and Bassett (2024).

of causal systems are examined – these include the pathway and cascade concepts. The next section explores these two causal concepts and how they have unique features, are associated with distinct analogies, and are studied with particular causal investigative strategies. However, the analysis in the next section does not require that one commit to the narrow mechanism notion. If the broad notion of mechanism is preferred, then these three causal systems (which are called "mechanisms," "pathways," and "cascades" in this Element) can all be considered distinct types of causal mechanisms. The important point is not what we call these causal systems, per se, but that we have an account that captures the distinct features of these causal systems and different types of causal explanations they provide.

2.3 Pathways

When biologists and other life scientists provide causal explanations, what types of causal systems do they refer to? What causal language is important for capturing the causal systems they find explanatory? While "mechanism" is a common causal term and concept, many other causal concepts are found in these scientific fields. Examples of causal concepts in the life sciences include pathways, cascades, circuits, triggers, causal cycles, and structuring causes. This subsection examines the pathway and cascade concepts. I argue that pathways and cascades differ from mechanisms in terms of their characteristic or hallmark features, the analogies they are associated with, and the causal investigative strategies used to study them. This analysis is used to suggest that explanations that appeal to pathways, cascades, and mechanisms are distinct types of explanation because they cite different types of causal systems.

A first causal concept to consider is the notion of a pathway, which is commonly found in biology, neuroscience, physiology, ecology, and numerous other life sciences (Boniolo and Campaner 2018; Ross 2018). Examples of the pathway concept include gene expression pathways, metabolic pathways, neural pathways, vascular pathways, developmental pathways, and ecological pathways, as seen in Figure 7. In these contexts, pathways are causal systems that have four main features. These features include: a sequence of causal steps, the flow of information or material, abstraction from causal detail, and causal relationships that emphasize causal connection (as opposed to mechanical interactions) (Ross 2021a). Additionally, while mechanisms are often analogized to machines, pathways have their own unique analogy – pathways are often analogized to roadways, highways, and city streets. The reasons for this analogy will become clear as the main features of the pathway concept are discussed in detail.

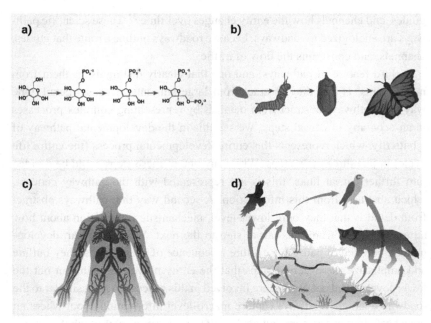

Figure 7 Pathway examples in the life sciences, including (a) metabolic pathways, (b) developmental pathways, (c) vascular pathways (or blood vessels), and (d) ecological pathways (which capture prey–predator relationships).

A first feature of pathways is that they involve a sequence of causal steps – these steps outline a causal route from upstream, to intermediate, to downstream factors.[30] In their simplest form, pathways are linear but they can be organized in more complex branching configurations. This sequential feature of pathways is seen in the butterfly developmental pathway in Figure 7, in which a sequence of causal steps – from egg to larvae, to pupa, to adult – is represented.

Second, pathways involve the flow of some entity along their sequence of causal steps. In many cases, pathways involve the flow of some material or information that is relevant to the system of interest. For example, metabolic pathways involve the flow of metabolites, neural pathways guide the flow of information, vascular pathways dictate the flow of blood, ecological pathways channel the flow of energy through ecosystems, and developmental pathways trace the flow of cells, tissues, or organisms, as they mature. In this manner, pathways involve both an entity that changes and a sequence of steps that limits,

---

[30] The relevant notion of order in pathways – used to clarify when a factor is upstream or downstream – is determined causally. Thus, pathways specify causal order (as opposed to mere temporal order).

guides, and channels how the entity changes over time.[31] These scientific pathways are analogized to roadways, because roadways outline a route that guides, channels, and constrains the flow of traffic.

A third feature of pathways, and one that clearly distinguishes them from mechanisms, is that they abstract from large amounts of causal detail. One way that pathways abstract from detail is by representing complex processes in an economy of causal steps. We see this in the developmental pathway of a butterfly, which represents this entire developmental process (the entire life cycle) in just three main steps. While any one of these steps could be divided into further causal links, this is not represented with the pathway concept, which abstracts from this information. A second way that pathways abstract from detail is that they omit lower-level, mechanistic information about how an entity moves from one causal step to the next. When vascular, developmental, and neural pathways capture a sequence of causal steps, they outline and emphasize the different steps that the entity moves through, but not the lower-level causal details that are involved in this process. Again, similar to the roadway analogy, roadways capture macro-level information about where an object can flow in a system, but not how it flows (or moves) through this space. A roadway reveals where cars can travel, but not the mechanistic details of how the car moves from one location to another. Similarly, metabolic pathways capture causal routes along which metabolites travel, but not the lower-level enzymatic details that drive this travel. For example, the glycolytic pathway captures a ten-step metabolic process that is shared and "conserved" across nearly all species on the planet. However, it is only the higher-level, causal steps outlined in the glycolytic pathway that are shared – this pathway is instantiated by different causal-mechanical details in different systems (such as different enzymes at a given step of the pathway). By abstracting from detail, the pathway can capture what all these systems share and it can explain the glycolytic process (conversion of glucose into pyruvate) generally, across all systems. Including lower-level mechanistic detail would prevent this, because such details are not shared across all systems.

A fourth feature of pathways is that their causal relationships emphasize causal connection, but not lower-level detail or mechanical detail. In other words, pathways capture *that* X is a cause of Y, but they do not reveal mechanistic details about *how* X causes Y. Their role is to highlight the set of causal connections in some domain – namely, who is causally connected to who, but not fine-grained information about these causal connections. For example,

---

[31] In some cases, pathways involve constraints that limit the possibility space of outcomes that a system can produce (Ross 2023b,c, 2024).

neural tracts can outline the flow of neural signals from one location to another, but they do not convey how these signals flow, travel, or move. This emphasis on causal connection with the pathway concept is seen when scientists organize many causal pathways together into network diagrams or what they sometimes call "roadmaps" of causal connections. This is seen in reference to "roadmaps" of metabolic pathways, "roadmaps" of stem cell developmental pathways, and "roadmaps" of ecological pathways (Marina et al. 2018; Ly et al. 2020; Zheng et al. 2021).

If pathways are unique causal systems, with the four features mentioned earlier, how do they provide explanations? How do pathways provide causal explanations that differ from mechanistic explanation? Consistent with the three-part model of explanation (shown in Figure 2), pathway explanations are cases in which pathways serve as the explanans and explain the outcome of interest. As pathways refer to a causal structure that differs from mechanisms, citing them provides a distinct type of causal explanation. On this view, one way to capture different types of causal explanations is by appreciating the distinct causal systems they cite that perform the explanatory "work." As mentioned earlier, consider explanations of glycolysis, which is a process by which organisms breakdown glucose into energy. When scientists explain glycolysis across a large number of species (or in living systems in general) they cite the "conserved" glycolytic pathway, with ten chemical conversion steps (from glucose to pyruvate). This pathway abstracts from lower-level mechanistic details, such as the enzymes that catalyze each step of the process. The reason for this abstraction is that the ten-step glycolytic pathway is shared across all systems in the explanatory target, while the lower-level enzymes are not. As the lower-level mechanisms in these systems are not shared, they cannot be cited to explain their identical behavior of glucose production. Similar reasoning is found in many explanations in biology (Sober 1999; Ross 2020) and in explanations of shared or universal behaviors across systems that differ in terms of their lower-level details (Batterman 2001; Ross 2015; Woodward 2017).

Another way to see the uniqueness of pathway explanations is with the network and "roadmap" diagrams of pathways. Consider the map of ecological pathways, shown in Figure 7. These pathway maps allow scientists to answer unique explanatory why-questions that mechanisms do not address. These explanatory why-questions include: (1) Given a starting point on the map, which downstream locations can (and cannot) be reached? (2) Given a downstream location, which upstream positions can (and cannot) arrive at this location? (3) What is the most (and least) direct way to get from any two points in the map? While there are other questions that this pathway map can answer, the important point is showing how pathway information helps scientists answer distinct types of explanatory why-questions. The questions here concern a possibility-space of outcomes and how an entity moves through this space. This matters for determining the flow of toxins as they damage species in an ecosystem, how blood clots move through blood vessels to damage some organs in the body (and not others), and how to manufacture particular chemical species from available chemical reactions (Ross 2021a, 2023b). Examining these pathway maps makes it clear that they do not represent mechanistic information – these maps do not represent a mechanism, in the sense of lower-level causal parts (or gears) that interact together to produce a single outcome of the system. Instead, these pathway maps capture a possibility space of routes in the system that capture where some entity can and cannot flow through this space. While pathways provide dynamic information about possible outcomes within a complex space, mechanisms explain why a particular, specific outcome presents.

Finally, in addition to their four main features, pathways are studied with unique causal investigative strategies. Scientists often study these systems by exploiting their "flow" feature. In particular, they often use tags and tracers to mark some entity, and then watch it as it flows along the steps of the pathway. This is seen in radioactive tracer and dye experiments, in which these materials are used to illuminate the steps of many different types of pathways, including metabolic, vascular, neural, and ecological (Ross 2021b). For example, radioactive tracers are attached to carbon atoms that flow through metabolic pathways, radioactive tracers are introduced into prey and followed through prey–predator relationships in ecosystems, and dyes are attached to material that flows through neural pathways and tracts (Ross 2021b). These are not techniques that can always or easily be used with mechanisms, because many of them lack the reliable flow of some entity through their causal steps. This is similar to the gears of a watch mechanism – while these gears are involved in the causal process, there is no material that reliably moves along them (from the first gear, through all intervening gears, to the final time keeping behavior of interest). However, for metabolic, vascular, and ecological pathways, there are materials that reliably flow through the causal steps and that are targeted by tracers in the study of these systems. This reveals how these systems have distinct features that matter for how they are studied. Thus, while mechanisms are often studied by "drilling down," pathways are studied by dropping tags or tracers into a system and "expanding out" along causal routes. These tracers reveal the causal sequences of interest in some domain, but not the fine-grained, mechanical details of the causal routes of interest.

Before moving on, it might help to consider some objections that mechanists have voiced toward viewing pathways as an explanatory causal structure. Does the sparse detail of pathways make them less explanatory than mechanisms? Are pathways mere mechanism sketches that should be suffused with more detail in order to explain? These points are supported by Craver and Darden (2013) who consider pathways to be explanatorily deficient due to their lack of detail. They associate pathways with the "vice of chainology," in which "one becomes fascinated by nodes in a causal chain but loses sight of how the nodes work to produce, underlie, or maintain the phenomenon" (Craver and Darden 2013, 91). Along these lines, they claim that pathways are causal structures that are "incomplete" and that they reflect a "shallowness" of understanding (Craver and Darden 2013, 91–92).

These statements misunderstand scientists' use of the pathway concept and its explanatory role. The sparse nature of pathways is central to their explanatory power because it captures shared higher-level causal connections across systems with different lower-level details (Ross 2020). This is seen in explanations of glycolysis and other cases in which shared behaviors present across systems that differ in terms of their mechanistic details. In addition to capturing shared, macro-level details, pathways also capture distinct types of causal details, as seen in the "roadmaps" of causal connections. Mechanisms are equipped to capture lower-level causes that produce a particular behavior of interest, but they are not suited to capture a map of possible causal routes through a system. For this type of causal information, the pathway concept is much better-suited, as is the analogy of these pathways to roadways, highways, and city streets. Here we see that mechanisms are limited, not just because they involve lower-level details that we do not need, but because mechanisms do not capture information about flow and possible routes, which is required for some explanatory why-questions. Further varieties of causal (and non-causal) explanation are considered in the next subsection and section.

2.4 Cascades

Another causal concept that commonly figures in explanations in biology and many other scientific domains is the notion of a cascade (Ross In Press). Examples of cascades are plentiful in science – they include cell signaling cascades in physiology, trophic cascades in ecology, ischemic cascades in neuroscience, cascading reactions in physics and chemistry, and cascading disasters (or failures) in the social sciences, as seen in Figure 8 (Macfarlane 1966; Ripple et al. 2016; Smolyak et al. 2020). Similar to mechanisms and pathways, cascades are causal structures with unique features, analogies, and causal investigative

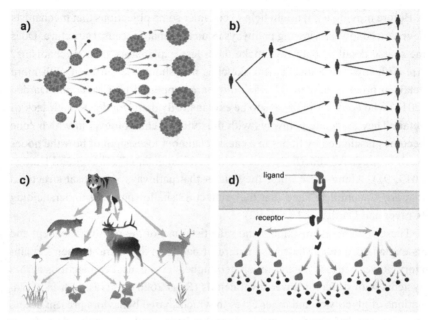

Figure 8 Cascade examples, including (a) cascading reactions in physics and chemistry, (b) cascading disease spread in epidemiology, (c) ecological cascades, and (d) cell-signaling cascades.

methods. Cascades have three main features: they involve an initial trigger, sequential amplification, and stable progression. In examining cascades in science it will help to introduce them with the analogies they are associated with. Cascades are often analogized to systems such as the snowball effect, ripple effect, and waterfalls (synonymous with "cascades," their namesake). We see why this is the case, by exploring their features more next.

First, cascades are initiated by a trigger, which is often conceptualized as a binary switch (on/off) that sets the process off. In order to see this, consider one of the first causal systems to receive the "cascade" label in modern biology, namely, the blood coagulation cascade (Davie and Ratnoff 1964; Macfarlane 1966). Blood coagulation is a process that functions to stop massive bleeding after blood vessel injury – this injury triggers an enzyme cascade, which culminates in a large clot to stop the bleeding. The trigger for blood coagulation is this vessel injury, which initiates the cascade process. Other examples of triggers in cascades are seen in the causal systems they are analogized to. The snowball effect is triggered by a small amount of snow, the ripple effect is triggered by a single drop of water, and waterfalls (or natural cascades) begin with a small amount of upstream water, which progressively disperses.

Second, the central feature of cascades is sequential amplification, which involves a small cause that produces an increasingly large amount of some effect.[32] At the scale of a single causal step, there are at least two types of causal amplification: a small amount of cause can produce a large amount of a single effect, called *single-product amplification*, or a small cause can produce many different effect types, called *multi-product amplification* (Ross In Press). An example of single product amplification is seen in enzyme cascades, such as the blood coagulation cascade, as these involve a small amount of some enzyme "a" that produces a large amount of downstream enzyme "b". In this enzyme case, there is amplification of a single product, as there is a large amount of enzyme "b." An example of multiproduct amplification is a disaster cascade, such as when an earthquake causes many different downstream outcomes, such as fires, collapsing bridges, and water damage from broken water pipes. In this disaster cascade, there is amplification in the sense of the production of many different types of effects.

While these two types of amplification help capture the notion of causal amplification at a single step, cascades involve *sequential* amplification, in which there are a sequence of amplifying steps. This is important because when amplifiers are arranged in series, this drastically increases the overall amplification of the system – the overall amplification of the system is the product of the gain at each step. For example, if one unit of enzyme "a" produces ten units of enzyme "b" and one unit of enzyme "b" produces ten units of enzyme "c," the overall process has a gain of one hundred (producing one hundred units of "c" for every single unit of "a"). This allows blood coagulation and other physiological cascades to produce "explosive" outcomes in which colossal amounts of a product are produced. In some cases, this amplification serves a physiological function, such as clot formation in the blood coagulation cascade and signal amplification in hormonal cascades. These cascades are also exploited in various technologies, such as polymerase-chain reaction (which amplifies trace amounts of some substance). In other cases, the amplification is non-functional and produces significant damage, as seen in ischemic cascades, disaster cascades, and cascading failures (Smolyak et al. 2020).

The sequential amplification feature of cascades is seen in the analogies they are associated with and the diagrams used to represent them. Notice that the cascade analogies all involve a small cause that amplifies a downstream effect.

---

[32] As seen in the examples here, a cause or effect is "small" or "large" relative to the units of interest (or choice of variable and values selected by scientists). This depends on the units specified, such as molecules of an enzyme in the blood coagulation cascade, or snow amount at steps along an avalanche.

For example, the snowball effect refers to a small amount of snow that causes a huge avalanche, the ripple effect involves a small drop that produces outward ripples that increase in size, and waterfalls involve a narrow stream of water that progressively amplifies in speed and distribution of spread. In analogizing scientific cascades to these systems, a main goal is to highlight and communicate the amplification in these causal systems. This amplification feature is also emphasized in the diagrams used to represent scientific cascades. These diagrams often depict one-to-many causal systems, in which one cause gives rise to many effects in succession (this is seen in the illustrations in Figure 8). Interestingly, as the degree of amplification (or gain) at any given step of the cascade is larger than can be easily drawn, scientists find other ways to represent this significant amplification (sometimes by representing the amplification numerically, with a 10^3 at a given step).

A third feature of cascades is that once initiated they involve stable progression to their final effect. In other words, cascades gain in momentum and are propelled forward as they move through their sequence of causal steps (Dodge et al. 2009). One implication of this is that, once initiated, cascades can be very difficult to stop. They have the potential to "run-away" or "become uncontrolled" (Bloomfield and Stephens 1996, 168, 171). This is similar to descriptions of the snowball effect, in which a small snow fall triggers a growing, unavoidable avalanche. As Stein states, "cascade refers to a process that once started, proceeds stepwise to its full, seemingly inexorable, conclusion [. . .] the danger of a cascade is that it can be inappropriately triggered [. . .] once triggered, it is virtually impossible to stop" (Stein 1990). This stable progression feature is seen in examples such as the initiation of a chemical chain reaction, the spread of COVID through the population, and cascading failures triggered by natural disasters. Due to this feature, scientists often recommend intervening early on in a causal cascade as a way to modify or stop it, as it becomes harder to control as its steps unfold.

If the narrow notion of mechanism is adopted (see Subsection 2.2), the cascade concept is an additional alternative to mechanism. In order to see this, consider that cascades do not always have the hierarchical organization of mechanisms (in which lower-level causes produce a higher-level effect). Cascades are level-agnostic with respect to their causes and effects. Cascades can have causes and effects at the same level, they can have higher-level causes that produce lower-level effects, and they can have lower-level causes that produce higher-level effects. Enzymatic cascades are an example of the first type (causes and effects at the same level) as the cause and effect are both enzymes. An example of higher-level causes producing lower-level effects are energy cascades involved in turbulence, which involve the transfer of energy from "large scales of motion to the small scales" ((Richardson 1922, 66); see also Wilson (2021)). Yet another example are traumatic experiences that alter gene expression, referred to as "downward cascades" (Masten and Cicchetti 2010, 492). Finally, a cascade example with a lower-level cause that produces a higher-level effect is a hormone cascade, in which a hormone trigger produces some system-level behavior. Another example is a pharmacological intervention that alters behavior, sometimes called an "upward cascade" (Masten and Cicchetti 2010 2010, 492).

Yet another difference between cascades and mechanisms is that unlike mechanisms, cascades do not always have a single, main effect of interest. Recall that the decomposition and localization methods used to study mechanisms require first fixing a single explanatory target before "drilling down" to identify the causal parts of the system. Cascades cannot be reliably studied in this way because they often have many distinct effects, as seen in multiproduct amplification cases. Furthermore, even when cascades do have a single main explanatory target, their causes cannot always be identified by "drilling down" because, as just mentioned, their causes are not always at lower-levels. Instead, cascades are often studied with tools that intervene on their initial trigger, using this as a way to study what their downstream effects are.

Finally, even if a broad notion of mechanism is adopted – such that the aforementioned cascade and pathway examples are said to count as mechanisms – it will still be important to distinguish across kinds of mechanisms. As suggested in this analysis, these varieties of causal systems (whatever they are called) have different features that set them apart from each other, require different causal investigative strategies, provide different types of control over effects, and figure in distinct types of explanations. Capturing the nuanced picture of causal varieties in the world and types of causal explanations in science requires a framework that appreciates these distinct causal systems.

2.5 Causal Explanation Conclusions

Providing an account of causal explanation in biology and the life sciences requires specifying the types of causal structures that scientists cite in their explanations. These causal structures serve as the explanans in the three-part model of explanation, and they capture what does the explanatory "work" in these cases. The analysis in this section is compatible with the claim that "causes explain their effects." What is highlighted is that there are many distinct types of causes and causal systems that play this explanatory role. Referring to all of these explanatory causal systems as "mechanisms" involves adopting a broad, expansive notion of mechanism, on which mechanism is synonymous with "causal system." As others have voiced, while it may be possible to "shoe-horn descriptions of biological systems into talk of mechanisms," the "attempt to do so risks reducing the idea of a mechanism to vacuity" (Dupré 2013).[33] Alternatively, referring to particular causal systems as mechanisms adopts a narrow notion of mechanism – a notion in which "mechanism" refers to causal systems with specific features. Whichever view of "mechanism" one adopts, the important point is that different types of causes, causal relationships, and causal systems are explanatory. Identifying and distinguishing these causal types is an important part of providing an account of scientific explanation that captures work in biology and the life sciences.

3 Non-Causal, Mathematical Explanation

When the deductive-nomological (DN) model of scientific explanation was revealed as having various limitations, causal accounts of scientific explanation began to receive increasing amounts of attention (Woodward and Ross 2021). One reason for this increased attention to causal explanation is that many problems with DN explanation were resolved by including causal details and information.[34] This perceived importance of causality in explanation led many to suggest that causal explanation is the main or only type of explanation in science (Lewis 1986; Strevens 2008; Skow 2014). As work on causal explanation began to develop further – in terms of specifying the features, types, and limits of causal explanation – many began to question claims that all scientific explanations are causal in character. Various philosophers began to claim that some genuine scientific explanations are non-causal or mathematical (Sober 1983; Batterman 2001; Baker 2005; Lange 2018). A large number of projects have focused on clarifying the structure of non-causal, mathematical explanations, including: the particular types of non-causal, mathematical factors these explanations involve, what exactly makes these factors explanatory, and whether there are different types of non-causal, mathematical explanations in science.

In the context of debates concerning scientific explanation, accounts of non-causal, mathematical explanation often adhere to various standards.[35] First,

---

[33] Another worry is that, on these broad accounts, "it seems that mechanisms just are whatever explains whatever happens" (Dupré 2013).

[34] For example, including causal information helped address issues concerning asymmetries and irrelevancies.

[35] In referring to explanations in this section as "non-causal, mathematical" I do not mean to suggest that all non-causal explanations are mathematical. I use this expression to highlight two main features of the explanations discussed in this work, namely, their non-causal nature and that they involve explanatory mathematics.

these accounts are focused on explanations of natural phenomena – they are focused on the use of mathematics (or non-causal information) in natural science explanations or explanations of the physical world. Expressed in a different way, these accounts are not interested in mathematical explanations in the field of mathematics or in non-scientific domains (Baker 2005). Additionally, many of these philosophical accounts of non-causal, mathematical explanation aim to capture explanatory reasoning found in scientific work. As Lange notes, this is a view of scientific explanation that aims to "do justice to scientific practice" (Lange 2018, 24). This requires identifying explanatory targets of scientific interest, such that these targets can be couched in explanatory why-questions and then answered, as opposed to providing obscure mathematical answers to previously unknown and scientifically uninteresting questions (Baker 2005).

A second important standard that these accounts of non-causal, mathematical explanation are held to is that they need to justify the explanatory role of mathematics. It is well appreciated that mathematics is used to represent phenomena in the world. However, while this representational capacity can support the scientific aims of description, prediction, and classification, these are all distinct from explanation. This is why these cases are often referred to as "distinctively mathematical" – they are not just explanations that "employ" mathematics, but cases in which the mathematics has the special feature of being explanatory (Lange 2018, 4). A convincing argument for the explanatory nature of mathematics must address this question of explanatory power and demonstrate how the math is doing more than merely representing phenomena in the world. Finally, most accounts of non-causal, mathematical explanation do not claim to be entirely free of causal information. While these explanations often have some causal information, it is argued that they *require* non-causal, mathematical information to be explanatory. In these accounts, there is some mathematical (or non-causal) kernel required for the complete explanation that marks it as distinct from standard causal explanations.

The topic of non-causal, mathematical explanation has received growing attention for different reasons. One reason stems from concerns that philosophical accounts of scientific explanation have overlooked non-causal, mathematical explanation and focused mainly (or exclusively) on causal explanation (Lange 2018). Work in this area aims to correct this deficiency by clarifying how non-causal, mathematical explanations should be understood and how they work. A second reason for attention to this topic concerns debates about the existence of mathematical objects and so-called "indispensability arguments" that argue in favor of this existence (Baker 2005; Lyon and Colyvan 2008; Lyon 2012). In these debates, Platonists argue that mathematical objects exist by showing that mathematics is indispensable to scientific explanation of the physical world. As Maddy states, according to a simple indispensability argument "we have good reason to believe our best scientific theories, and mathematical entities are indispensable to those theories, so we have good reason to believe in mathematical entities" (Maddy 1992, 278). On the other hand, nominalists deny the existence of mathematical objects and find ways to refute these Platonist arguments. These discussions center on whether "pure mathematics can be genuinely explanatory with respect to physical phenomena" as this is viewed as having consequences for whether we accept the existence of mathematical entities or not (Baker 2005, 225).

In this Element, analysis of non-causal, mathematical explanation will focus on the first motivation, namely, on an interest in mathematical explanation for the sake of clarifying how legitimate scientific explanations work. As all explanations discussed in this section are non-causal in character and have mathematical components, the terms "non-causal explanation" and "mathematical explanation" will be used interchangeably. This section will focus on three categories of mathematical explanation: (i) topological and constraint-based explanations, (ii) optimality and efficiency explanations, and (iii) minimal model explanations. While these are three common types of mathematical explanation, I will not suggest that these categories are exhaustive of all forms of mathematical explanation. Additionally, while these categories of mathematical explanation are marked by distinct features (with paradigmatic cases in each category), this analysis is open to "boarder-line" cases, in which a mathematical explanation may share features from more than one of these categories. This analysis will also reveal some similarities between previously discussed causal explanations and the non-causal, mathematical explanations examined here.

This section will examine the structure of these explanation types, how they capture the explanatory role of mathematics, and how they fit with the standard three-part model of explanation, which includes the explanandum, explanans, and dependency relation.

3.1 Topological and Constraint-Based Explanations

A first type of non-causal, mathematical explanation are topological explanations. These explanations are commonly found in network and systems science areas, in which life science cases are studied with network models, graph theory, and pathway analysis. In these examples, systems are represented with network models containing nodes and edges – nodes capture properties in the system (metabolic compounds, areas of the brain, species in an ecosystem, etc.), while edges capture relations between these properties (chemical conversions, anatomical connections, prey–predator relations, etc.). In the context of network neuroscience, some of these models capture the brain's structural and anatomical connections, which are referred to as the brains "network architecture," "structural topology" and "hard-wired connection topology" (Zöller et al. 2021). Similar methods are used to represent networks in other domains, such as enzyme interactions in molecular biology, cellular interactions in immunology, prey–predator relationships in ecology, and many others (Montoya and Solé 2002; Kitano and Oda 2006; Taylor et al. 2013). These network diagrams reveal the "global shape" of connections in some domain and, because of this, are also referred to as "circuit diagrams" and "wiring diagrams" of connections in the system (Karuza et al. 2016).

Representing systems with network and graphical formats can reveal important topological properties of the system. These topological properties capture how relations between entities in the system are arranged and organized – in this manner, the "topology of a graph defines how the links between system elements are organized" (Fornito et al. 2016). Examples of topological properties include: connection or linkage density, link distance number, small-worldness, nested relations, power-law scale-free distributions and scaling properties (Bassett and Bullmore 2017). In many cases, these topological properties are cited in explaining unique behaviors of the system. While these topological properties are sometimes characterized as "mathematical" themselves, they are also claimed to bear a mathematical relationship to the system-level behaviors that they produce. In this manner, it is suggested that there is a mathematical dependency relation between the topology of a system and the behavior produced.

As an introductory example, consider a topological explanation that is commonly discussed in the philosophical and mathematics literatures (Euler 1956; Pincock 2012; Lange 2018). While this example is not drawn from the life sciences, it motivates and captures an explanatory pattern that is identified in many life science contexts. This is the well-known case of the Königsberg bridges. In this example, a set of rivers runs through the eighteenth-century city of Königsberg, shown in Figure 9 (Adams and Franzosa 2008). In this layout, there are seven bridges that span the river, such that the two central islands are connected to surrounding land. According to this story, there was interest in determining whether it was possible to walk a path across each bridge exactly and only once. After much deliberation an answer was provided by Euler in the form of a mathematical proof. Euler represented the bridge system graphically, as shown in Figure 9, in which landmasses are represented as nodes and the bridges

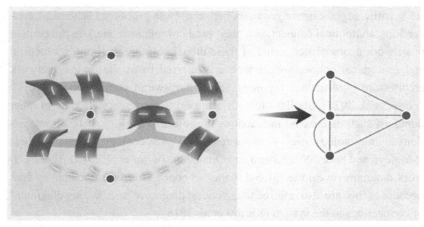

Figure 9 The Königsberg bridges. The figure on the left represents the seven Königsberg bridges, which cross different sections of river. This structure of bridges is represented graphically in the figure on the right, in which the landmasses are represented as nodes and the bridges as edges (Adams and Franzosa 2008).

as edges.[36] He used this graphical depiction to demonstrate that in order for there to be a walking path of this nature – what we now call an Eulerian path – two conditions needed to be met: (3.1a) all nodes should be connected and (3.1b) the amount of nodes with an odd number of connections (or edges) should be zero or two (Euler 1956; Ross 2021). In this example, the explanatory why-question is "In the Königsberg bridge case, is it possible to walk across each bridge exactly and only once?"[37] Importantly, the answer to this question is "no," and the explanation of this is provided by mathematics, in particular the mathematical proof and failure to meet both conditions mentioned earlier (3.1a, 3.1b).

This example is viewed as a non-causal explanation for a number of reasons. First, the causal properties and constituents of the bridges are irrelevant to the explanation – all the matters is the macroscale topology of the system. If the same arrangement of bridges is present, but you change the lower-level materials they are made of (steel, iron, wood, etc.) the explanation still holds (Pincock 2012). The topological structure lacks lower-level physical-causal details, but it also lacks causal details at macro-scales. As Huneman states, this type of "topological explanation" is one that "abstracts away from causal relations and

---

[36] This is now considered some of the earliest work in graph theory and topology.

[37] This explanatory why-question can be rephrased as "Does this system have an Eulerian path or not?"

interactions in a system, in order to pick up some sort of 'topological' properties of that system and draw from those properties mathematical consequences that explain the features of the system they target" (Huneman 2010, 214). In this example, math is used to capture abstract features of the system that are explanatory and independent of causal details. Second, not only does the explanans (the topological structure) have a mathematical character in this case, but the dependency relation in this explanation is mathematical as well. This explanation contains a dependency relation between topological properties (meeting the two criteria mentioned earlier) and presence of an Eulerian path. Whether an Eulerian path is present or not depends on the topology of the system. However, in the Königsberg case, this dependency relation is mathematical and not causal (Woodward 2019). Causal dependencies have an empirical character that mathematical dependencies lack. Causal dependencies require empirical study to be identified and studied in the world. Identifying that a gene, drug, or vitamin deficiency causes some outcome requires empirical study in the world and cannot be revealed by mathematics alone (proofs, derivations, etc.). However, for the Königsberg case and others, once the topological features of the system are identified, mathematical understanding alone can reveal consequences of the system and answer explanatory why-questions. In these examples, topological properties have "mathematical consequences" that power the explanation, as opposed to causal consequences that require empirical discovery (Huneman 2010).

Consider similar explanations in the context of ecology and neuroscience. A first example involves explanations of ecosystem robustness in the face of species extinctions. An ecosystem's prey–predator relationships can be represented with graphical models, in which nodes represent different species and edges capture the relations between species. With this graphical model, the extinction of species from the ecosystem can be represented with the deletion of nodes. One way to explain the robustness of an ecosystem to species extinction is to determine how the system responds to random deletions to nodes in the network. In this case, topological properties of the network can explain whether the ecosystem will be stable (or robust) in the face of a random node deletion in the network. In particular, if the graph has a scale-free or small world structure, in which there are few highly connected nodes, the system is more stable as a less-connected node is more likely to be deleted (Huneman 2010; Ross 2021). Removing a less-connected node is less disturbing to the network than removing a highly connected node. Alternatively, if a system lacks this scale-free structure (and has many highly connected nodes) a random deletion is more likely to hit a highly connected node, which would lead to more disruption and instability. Similar to the Königsberg case, explaining why a system is more or less robust has to do with abstract, topological features of the system and not with the system's physical constituents, realizers, or higher-scale causal connections. This allows the same explanation to be provided for other systems that share the same topological structure, even when they differ in terms of lower-level and causal details.

Other examples of topological explanation are found in neuroscience, such as those involving human brain networks and neural networks of model organisms, such as *C. elegans*. Studies of the *C. elegans* neural network reveals a "small-world" network topology characterized by high clustering and a short path length (Watts and Strogatz 1998). This small-world "connection topology" – found in *C. elegans*, other living organisms, and various non-living systems – has been cited in explaining particular behaviors, such as signal-propagation speed, computational power, and synchronizability (Watts and Strogatz 1998, Bassett and Bullmore 2017). In other cases, the small-world structure of neural networks is cited in explaining the economical character of the system, in the sense of minimizing biological costs, while maximizing topological integration (Bassett and Bullmore 2017).[38] These explanations fit the non-causal category because the explanatory target of interest – unique behaviors of the system – are a mathematical consequence of the system's topology, as opposed to an empirically identified cause-effect relationship. In these explanations, the "abstract, dimensionless" topological features are unique in that they "tell us nothing about the physical layout" of the nervous system or how it is "embedded in anatomical space" (Bassett and Bullmore 2017).

All three of these examples – the Königsberg, ecological, and neural network cases – share explanatory features. Each of these cases specifies how the topology of the system (the explanans) "makes a difference' to the system's behavior (the explanandum), in which this difference-making relation (dependency relation) is specified mathematically. In these cases, the explanatory work is supplied by topological properties, which abstract from lower-level and causal details. The fact that these explanations abstract from lower-level details, gives them the ability to generalize across microstructurally distinct systems. A system's scale-free structure explains its robustness across contexts – this explanation holds in the contexts of enzyme networks, cellular networks, brain networks, ecological networks, social networks, and so on. This captures the global and domain-general nature of these explanations, as the same topological properties can be instantiated by different lower-level details.

---

[38] In this case, biological costs include the costs of maintaining physical connections and communication between nodes.

While these topological cases are examples of non-causal explanation, this does not mean that topology only explains in a non-causal manner. In some situations, topology can capture higher-level causal connections in a system, which provide causal explanations (Ross 2021). Examples of these causal topologies include the bowtie (fan-in, fan-out) network structure of human immune cell interactions, the chokepoint topology in enzyme networks, and unique connection topologies in ecosystem networks (Ross 2021). The abstraction involved in both the non-causal and causal topological explanations captures their autonomy from lower-level detail and their domain general character. After significant emphasis on reductive explanation in the philosophical literature, these cases have proved helpful in demonstrating the rationale behind non-reductive explanations and cases in which macro-scale structures have explanatory power.

These non-causal topological explanations are related to another account of non-causal explanation that Lange refers to as "explanations by constraint" (Lange 2018, 3). Lange provides an account of non-causal explanation, in which factors are explanatory in virtue of the fact that they constrain the system in some way. Notice that in the Königsberg bridge case, the topology is explanatory in virtue of its constraining influence on potential walking paths. Lange elaborates on this to identify two important features of these explanations. First, these constraint-based explanations are non-causal because (i) the constraining influence of mathematics is stronger than causal influence. The strength of the constraining influence in these mathematical explanations, sets them apart from the weaker causal influence found in causal explanations. In this manner, mathematical explanations have a stronger form of necessity than causal relationships – this allows mathematical explanations to show why an outcome "was inevitable to a stronger degree than could result from the action of causal powers" (Lange 2018, 6). Second, (ii) the strength of the constraining influence of the explanatory mathematics in these cases allows them to provide a unique type of "impossibility" explanation. These explanations do not just show why some outcomes are not realized, but why it is strictly impossible for them to occur. This is intended to capture how the Königsberg topology has explanatory impact that is stronger than causality and how it explains why it is impossible to take an Eulerian path in the system.

Lange uses these two features (i, ii) to identify other non-causal explanations, which need not involve topology. Consider a non-scientific explanation that illustrates this: suppose a mother has twenty-three strawberries and she wants to divide them evenly among her three children. What explains why this is impossible? According to Lange, this impossibility is explained by mathematical facts and it does not have to do with causal relationships in the world. While causal relationships have influence over which outcome of a set of possible outcomes manifests, they lack the strong form of necessity implied by the explanatorily relevant mathematics in these cases. The strong type of necessity in these mathematical explanations is what allows them to explain impossibilities – not just why something did not happen, but why it could not possibly happen at all. As Lange states, "[t]he Königsberg bridges as so arranged were never crossed because they *couldn't* be crossed. Mother's strawberries were not distributed evenly among her children because they *couldn't* be" (Lange 2018, 9).

Consider a similar non-causal explanation from the contexts of human genetics. In humans, genes contain four different types of nucleotides (A,C,T,G), which are arranged linearly in DNA. When genes are expressed to produce proteins, these nucleotides are "read" sequentially, three at a time. Each three nucleotides in a gene – referred to as a "codon" – codes for a particular amino acid, which are small units that make-up proteins. Scientific research has revealed which three-nucleotide sequences (codons) code for particular amino acids and it has become clear that there are only 64 possible codons in humans. What explains this limit on codon types? If our explanatory-why question is, "Why are there 64 possible codons in humans as opposed to more or less?" the answer to this is provided by mathematics. The fact that there are only four nucleotide options, which are organized in sequences of three, mathematically entails that there are 64 possibilities (as 4^3 or $4 \times 4 \times 4 = 64$).[39] In this case, the explanatory power is not derived from causality, but from mathematics. The mathematics explains why there are exactly 64 possibilities and why it is impossible for there to be more. In other words, the math constrains possible codon number and it explains why it is impossible to have more than 64 codon types in humans. Similar to the Königsberg, ecological, and neuroscience examples, there are some empirical facts that are accepted when formulating the explanatory why-question. However, the answer to this question is provided from mathematical derivation alone and not empirical-causal assessment. There are surely other types of these mathematical, impossibility explanations in the life sciences. In exploring these types, it will be fruitful to focus on cases that matter to scientists, that they view as furthering their understanding of the natural world, and that capture their explanatory practices, aims, and goals.

---

[39] Consider the three positions in the nucleotide code – for the first position there are four options (A,C,T,G), for the second there are four options again, and same for the third position. This means that there are $(4 \times 4 \times 4 = 64)$ 64 different (three nucleotide) codon possibilities. These 64 different codons do not all code for unique amino acids – some of them have overlap and code for the same ones. There are about 20 different amino acids (that are coded for in humans).

This analysis reveals overlap and dissimilarities between two accounts of non-causal explanations, namely, topological and constraint-based explanations. Both explanation types involve a mathematical explanans and a mathematical dependency relation. Differences include the fact that sometimes the explanatory math is topological, while other times it is not (such as in the strawberry and genetics examples). Furthermore, both types contain some impossibility explanations (as seen in the Königsberg and genetics examples), but in topological cases there is sometimes more interest in explaining unique behaviors of the system (such as fragility, robustness, energy costs, etc.) as opposed to whether an outcome is impossible or possible for the system.

3.2 Optimality and Efficiency Explanations

A second main category of non-causal, mathematical explanation are optimality or efficiency explanations, which often arise in the context of evolutionary biology. Modern interest in these cases is motivated by indispensability arguments and attempts to capture the diversity of explanatory practice in science (Baker 2005; Lyon and Colyvan 2008; Lyon 2012; Pincock 2012; Lange 2013). Many of these cases involve surprising traits in organisms, which are explained by appealing to mathematical considerations. Examples of these surprising traits include explaining why cicadas emerge on prime-number-year life cycles, why honeybees have hexagonal-shaped honeycombs, and why sunflower seeds are arranged according to a Fibonacci-sequence (or Golden ratio) on the heads of sunflowers (Baker 2005; Lyon and Colyvan 2008; Ross 2023c). For many of these cases, the explanation involves two main components: (i) a background assumption that evolutionary processes select traits that are more efficient, optimal, or advantageous for the individual or species, and (ii) an argument – often mathematical – for how the trait in question meets this standard of being more efficient, optimal, or advantageous. The point is not that these explanations lack causal information – they clearly include this by appealing to evolutionary processes. The claim is that the explanatory work is not provided by causality alone, as it also requires mathematics.

Optimality and efficiency explanations build on the structure of the previous topological and constraint-based explanations in an important way. While cases in the previous subsection explained the system's behavior by appealing to its mathematical features, the explanations in this subsection explain the *presence* of mathematical features in the system by appealing to the evolutionary advantage that these mathematical features convey.[40] The similarity is that

---

[40] One implication of this is that some of the topological explanations in the last subsection can be converted into optimality/efficiency explanations if the focus is on explaining why the system

explanations in this and the last subsection capture how mathematical features have particular consequences for the system – the difference is that explanations in this subsection use these consequences to explain why the mathematical features are present in the system. As will be discussed more soon, optimality and efficiency explanations share a similar structure to "existence" or functional explanations, which explain the existence of some property in a system on the basis of the consequence it produces or entails (Wright 1976).

A first example of optimality and efficiency explanations is the case of cicada life cycles. Cicadas are insects that spend part of their life cycle underground as nymphs, after which they emerge on predictable intervals. One species of cicada (the *Magicicada* genus) reliably emerges on intervals of prime number years – in particular 13 and 17 years – and there is interest in explaining why this is the case (Baker 2005, 230). To be clear, there is interest in explaining why these cicadas emerge on prime number years as opposed to more common non-prime number year intervals. Explanations of this prime number year emergence are provided by the fact that prime number life cycles reduce the cicadas overlap with predator species. It is suggested that the evolutionary advantage of this reduced overlap has led to the selection and permanence of this prime number year life cycle.

The mathematical component of this explanation requires explaining why prime numbers reduce predator overlap. This explanation is provided by the notion of the lowest common multiple (lcm) within number theory in mathematics, as this shows how the frequency of intersection is minimized with prime numbers (Baker 2005, 230–232). Given that cicadas can have life cycles between thirteen and 18 years (due to ecological constraints), this is the age range that is considered. In considering this range, the advantage of primes is evident by the mathematical fact that "12 (a non-prime) intersects with 1, 2, 3, 4, and 6; while 13 (a prime) only intersects with 1" (Lyon 2012, 561). For these reasons, mathematics, and number theory in particular, are said to play "a genuinely explanatory role in accounting for the cycle lengths of periodical cicadas" (Baker 2005, 237). The mathematics in this case helps explain why "primes are optimal," which is necessary to explain why they have been selected through evolutionary processes (Baker 2005, 232).

In considering the structure of this explanation, it helps to examine the role of the mathematics involved. The explanatory target in this case is presented as the prime number year life cycle of cicadas. In traditional accounts of

---

evolved to have the topological properties in question. Examples of this can be seen in neuroscience research that considers how "selection pressures might be operative on the evolution and development of nervous systems" and how "brain networks have been selected" to have various features (Bassett and Bullmore 2017).

scientific explanation, one selects the explanatory target and then identifies factors "upstream" of this target that account for, produce, or cause the target, and that the target "depends" on. This captures the directionality of the explanation from explanans to explanandum. For this prime number year life cycle there are "upstream" evolutionary considerations that "selected" for this trait. However, these explanations also cite the prime number year as an "upstream" factor that has mathematical consequences for the "downstream" outcome of species intersection frequency. This is natural because changing whether life cycles are prime or not "makes-a-difference" to and explains the degree of intersection in the species. And, relatedly, species intersection "depends" on presence of prime number year life cycle. However, this is somewhat nonstandard because it places the original explanatory target (prime number), in the upstream "explanans" position and the consequences of this math (the species intersection) in the downstream explanandum position. Interestingly, explaining primeness does not involve merely citing the upstream factors that selected it, but also appealing to its forward influence on the cicada species. The need to appeal to what produces and is produced by the prime-year life cycle makes this explanation unique.

This cicada example bears similarity to types of "functional explanation," in which one explains the existence of a biological trait on the basis of the trait's function in an organism or species (Wright 1973). In standard functional explanations, the link between the trait and the goal it serves is causal – for example, the heart exists in mammals because it causes the blood to circulate (and serves the function of blood circulation). As circulation is a subgoal that serves main goals of the organism (survival and reproduction), this explains the existence of the heart. The cicada example differs from this, in that the dependency relation between the prime-year life cycle and predator overlap is mathematical, as opposed to causal.[41] This mathematical dependency relation captures what is importantly non-causal and mathematical about this example, which distinguishes it from causal explanation.

A main question raised by this cicada example is how to integrate the mathematical and evolutionary components in the explanation. This explanation requires both components and they play different roles. One natural interpretation is to separate the explanation into two explanatory why-questions,

---

[41] What makes this dependency relation mathematical? This is supported by the fact that the relationship between prime years and predator overlap is revealed *a priori* through mathematics, and does not require empirical study of the world (which is the case for causal relationships) (Woodward 2019). This is related to discussion in subsection 1.2 regarding Hume's fork and different types of dependency relations in scientific explanations (Hume 1985; Woodward 2019).

which both need to be addressed. A first explanatory why-question is: Why do cicadas have the feature of prime-number year life cycles? Answer: Because this feature is evolutionarily efficient, optimal, or advantageous. A second explanatory why-question is: Why are prime-number year life cycles evolutionarily efficient, optimal, or advantageous? Answer: Because they reduce predator overlap, as explained by mathematical features of the least common multiple principle. The full explanation is not provided until both questions are answered, and they require causal and mathematical responses, respectively. While many philosophical accounts of evolutionary explanations assume that existing traits have been selected because they are optimal, efficient, or advantageous, this piece often requires careful justification (Wakil and Justus 2017).

Consider two further optimality explanations that fit a similar pattern. A second optimality explanation involves the explanatory why-question, "Why do bees have hexagonal-shaped honeycombs as opposed to honeycombs of other shapes?" The explanation of this geometrical trait involves a mathematical component revealing that hexagonal honeycombs are more efficient than other shapes because they use less honey and wax. The explanation of this optimality is provided by the honeycomb theorem, which "explains why a hexagonal grid is the optimal way to divide a surface up into regions of equal area" (Lyon and Colyvan 2008, Lyon 2012). The second piece is the evolutionary explanation, which specifies that this optimality makes these bees "fitter" and explains why the trait is selected for in the population. A third example is the Golden ratio spiral configuration of seeds on sunflower heads. Why do sunflowers pack their seeds in this configuration and not another? The answer here involves the fact that with this Golden ratio structure "the optimal packing of sunflower seeds is achieved" and that such optimality, due to the benefit it provides the species, is selected for through evolutionary processes. In both cases the mathematical trait makes a difference to some optimal outcome (less use of materials and higher packing density, respectively), and this difference is explained in virtue of mathematical relationships, dependencies, and information.

Other candidates for optimality and efficiency explanations are Sober's "equilibrium explanations" (Sober 1983), Chirimuuta's efficient coding explanations (Chirimuuta 2014), and Rice's discussion of various optimality explanations in biology (Rice 2015). Each of these cases explains an outcome by appealing to some evolutionary advantage – whether it is the "reproductive advantage" of a 1:1 sex ratio in a population, "evolutionary principles" that explain current behaviors such as the ability of neurons to "transmit more information," and other cases in which optimality models are used to "explain why a system has evolved the optimal strategy" (Sober 1983, Chirimuuta 2014, Rice 2015). While the optimality and efficiency explanations discussed in this section provide one class of non-causal, mathematical explanation, this does not imply that all evolutionary explanations or optimality explanations are non-causal. Some evolutionary explanations are causal in character and this framework is open to optimality and efficiency explanations outside of evolutionary biology.[42]

3.3 Minimal Model Explanations

A third class of non-causal mathematical explanations are "minimal model" explanations (Batterman 2002, 2021). These involve "minimal models," which abstract from various types of information, including causal detail, in order to have explanatory power. Batterman introduces this form of explanation by distinguishing two types of explanatory-why questions. The first is a type (i) why-question, which "asks for an explanation of why a given instance of some pattern obtained" (Batterman 2001, 23). The second is a type (ii) why-question, which "asks why, in general, patterns of a given type can be expected to obtain" (Batterman 2001, 23). In this manner, type (ii) why-questions ask why the same pattern is exhibited generally or universally across a large group of different systems.

Minimal model explanations provide answers to type (ii) why-questions – they aim to explain why behaviors generally obtain and why they are shared across distinct systems. In scientific contexts, these shared behaviors are captured with the notion of "universality" as they are universal behaviors that are shared across physically distinct systems (Kadanoff 1990; Batterman 2021). Examples of universal behaviors in the physical sciences include how the Navier-Stokes equations capture the behavior of many microstructurally distinct fluids, that physically distinct pendulums exhibit periods that are proportional to the square root of their length, and that systems as diverse as fluids and magnets exhibit identical behavior at their critical points (Batterman 2001; Batterman and Rice 2014). While Batterman's account of minimal model explanations was first examined in the context of physical science examples, later work applied his account to biological and life science explanations. Examples of universal behaviors in the life sciences include firing behaviors that are shared across physically distinct neurons (such as class I excitability), cases in which the same phenotype has different genetic and environmental causes (such as Parkinson's disease), and processes that are "conserved" across nearly all living systems (such as glycolysis). The central explanatory why-question in these contexts is why systems with different physical details all exhibit the same universal behavior.

---

[42] For an analysis of the role of optimality models in causal explanation, see Potochnik (2007).

Batterman suggests that universal behaviors are often explained with principled techniques that isolate a "minimal model," which is a model that "most economically caricatures the essential" features of the system (Goldenfeld 1992; Batterman 2001). In many of these explanations, mathematical techniques are used to remove irrelevant detail from models of distinct systems until the reduced models collapse into the same "minimal model" or the same "universality" class of models. Given that these techniques allow for the principled removal of detail – which preserves the qualitative behavior of systems – the fact that distinct systems are all reduced to the same model or class explains why they exhibit shared behavior. A main feature of these cases is the use of mathematical techniques in providing the explanation. While other mathematical explanations involve "mathematical entities" (a number, a graph, a geometrical feature, etc.), minimal model explanations involve an "essential operation" that is mathematical and does the explanatory work (Batterman 2010).[43]

Consider an example of the minimal model approach in neuroscience. In the mid-twentieth century, Hodgkin used voltage clamp studies of single crab neurons to identify three different types of neural excitability, referred to as class I, class II, and class III excitability (Hodgkin 1948). For class I neurons the frequency–current relationship increases continuously from zero, for class II neurons it is discontinuous, and for class III neurons it is undefined (Ross 2015, 40). Hodgkin identified that class I neurons are found in many different animals and it was later discovered that these neurons differ greatly in terms of their microstructural details. In order to appreciate this, consider mammalian pyramidal neurons, many of which exhibit class 1 behavior. These neurons have three main types of voltage-gated ion channels (selective for Na^+, K^+, and Ca^{2+}), and each of these can have hundreds of molecularly distinct subtypes. From this variety, each neuron can express over a dozen different types of voltage-gated ion channels and these vary in density along the membrane producing unique voltage-dependent conductances. This helps capture the vast molecular diversity of mammalian pyramidal neurons with this behavior – the diversity across all neurons with this behavior (beyond mammalian pyramidal neurons) is, of course, much greater.

Neuroscientists have been interested in explaining why neurons that differ in terms of their lower-level details all exhibit the same excitability behavior. A central component of this explanation was provided by Ermentrout and Kopell, who derived a canonical model for class I excitability (Hoppensteadt and Izhikevich 1997). This work involved using mathematical abstraction

---

[43] For example, some of the physical science examples that Batterman discusses involve renormalization group methods, as the mathematical technique in question.

procedures to condense models of molecularly diverse neural systems to a simple model, referred to as a canonical model. In this case, "when mathematical abstraction techniques are used to abstract away from details of mathematical representations of neural systems, all representations converge onto the same canonical model" (Ross 2015, 41). It is this convergence of the distinct models onto a shared single model that explains why they exhibit the same behavior despite their lower-level differences. In other words, because these mathematical reduction techniques eliminate detail while preserving qualitative behavior, the fact that all reduced models converge on the same model or class of models confirms and explains their qualitative similarity. This mathematical operation captures features of these systems that are "stable under perturbation of their microscopic details" (Batterman 2001).[44]

The minimal model account captures a non-reductive form of explanation that is supported by actual methods that scientists use in their work. Among the advantages of this explanatory framework is that it clarifies exactly why reductive forms of explanation are limited for particular explanatory targets. This limitation is that the shared, universal behavior of interest – that scientists want to explain – does not have a particular lower-level story, account, or explanation. In a line of reasoning that extends back to the work of Putnam (1967) and Fodor (1974) these shared behaviors are multiply-realized by different lower-level details, in a way that makes citing such lower-level details insufficient (Batterman 2001; Ross 2020). This is seen in cases in which the same metabolic pathway is instantiated by different lower-level enzymes, where the same bridge topology can have different lower-level material constituents, and where the same neural firing behavior is made-up of different ion channel details. This clarifies a strong problem with assuming that these explanatory targets should fit a reductive model of explanation. The next step in these cases, involves providing the principled rationale that guide which factors do (and do not) explain and what justifies this. Distinct strategies for finding and representing abstract features propose different frameworks to address this second question, from those that emphasize causal relevance and control, topological properties with pertinent consequences, and mathematical abstraction techniques that expose qualitative similarity.

3.4 Non-Causal Explanation Conclusions

The three types of non-causal explanation presented in this section have unique features, they share similarities, and sometimes the border between them is less distinct. Similar to minimal model explanations, topological explanations

---

[44] A similar attention to forms of explanation and understanding that involve abstracting from lower-level details is present in Green and Batterman (2017) and Batterman (2021).

abstract from large amounts of lower-level detail. In fact, it is a main feature of topological representations of systems that these representations are indifferent to lower-level, physical instantiations. This is what allows the same topology and explanation to capture neural networks in *C. elegans*, immune cell networks in humans, and social networks in societies. This is comparable to how the physical material of the Königsberg bridges are irrelevant to whether they have an Eulerian path or not. And a similar autonomy from lower-level details are found in some optimality and efficiency explanations. This is seen in Sober's equilibrium explanations for the 1:1 sex ratio in many species at reproductive age (Sober 1983). In this case, the 1:1 sex ratio is explained by showing "how the event would have occurred regardless of which of a variety of causal scenarios actually transpired" (Sober, 1983, 202). It is not factors in the actual causal history of any outcome that matter for these explanations – instead a variety of disjuncts captures possible outcomes, without the need to specify which actually occurs. Similarly, the mathematics underpinning the optimalities and efficiencies in the cicada, honeybee, and sunflower cases do not depend on or require particular lower-level details. The lowest common multiple principle, honeycomb proof, and Golden rule hold regardless of the details of the system. All accounts provide strong, principled reasons for why particular lower-level details are irrelevant to the explanation.

However, these types of non-causal explanation also differ in notable ways. Topological and constraint-based explanations tend to lean on coarse mathematical relationships, with little (to no) information about a system's goals or purposes. Unlike other forms of non-causal explanation, these include the unique impossibility explanations, which explain why some outcomes are impossible or off-limits for a system (Ross 2023c). Optimality and efficiency explanations, on the other hand, have the unique feature of including assumptions about a system's goals and how these are supported by the system's features. These are often found in evolutionary or design cases, in which there is interest in explaining why a system has a particular feature. Despite their differences, in many of these cases, insights into novel forms of explanation in biology and the life sciences have been provided by revealing unique types of explanatory targets and explanatory why-questions.

4 Final Remarks

The topic of scientific explanation continues to receive significant attention in the philosophical literature. Many continue to view explanation as a "distinctive aim" (Nagel 1961, 15) of science and one of its "primary objectives" (Hempel 1991, 299). Similar to work on scientific explanation in the mid to late twentieth century, current projects aim to identify the standards that genuine explanations should meet, they search for formal patterns that underlie explanatory practice, and they examine how well such projects include examples we take to be genuinely explanatory (while excluding cases we view as non-explanatory).

However, since this mid-to-late-twentieth-century work, while many questions about scientific explanation and basic orientations to them have stayed the same, philosophical accounts of scientific explanation have also changed in notable ways. First, while earlier accounts of scientific explanation had monist aspirations – attempting to capture the single structure of explanation and the "ideal form to which all efforts at explanation should strive" (Nagel 1961) – current accounts are much more pluralist in what they count as explanatory. Current accounts are generally open to scientific explanation having different forms, structures, and patterns. In fact, many novel accounts of scientific explanation use monist frameworks (such as the DN model or mechanistic explanation) as a foil for showing that other forms of explanation exist (Batterman 2001; Dupré 2013; Woodward and Ross 2021; Ross 2021a, In Press). Much current work appreciates that there are causal and non-causal forms of explanation, with subtypes in each category. This pluralistic orientation is often viewed as compatible with the fact that different scientific domains have unique explanatory situations, targets, and goals.

Second, while earlier explanatory frameworks were often reductive in character, current accounts accommodate non-reductive explanations. In earlier work, it was common to find claims that explanatory power tracks appeal to fundamental physics or increasingly lower-levels of detail (Salmon 1984; Sober 1999). However, these reductive claims have largely been replaced by views that this is not always so – that sometimes higher-level causes, factors, and concepts provide the best explanation (Weber 2008; Woodward 2017; Ross 2020). Such non-reductive accounts justify the explanatory power of higher-level factors, and they clarify why abstraction is required for understanding (Batterman 2010; Pincock 2012). Gaining clarity on these issues is consistent with accepting that principled forms of reductive explanation exist and are sometimes needed (Bickle 2006; Barwich 2021). This acknowledgment of reductive and non-reductive explanation in biology and the life sciences further illustrates the pluralistic point earlier. This pluralistic view suggests that the level or scale of explanatory detail is not always fixed and can differ from case to case, as dictated by principled considerations.

Third, it has grown increasingly common to expect philosophical accounts of scientific explanation to capture the actual work of scientists. This is an orientation to scientific explanation that requires close contact with the methods, reasoning, concepts, and strategies that scientist's use in their efforts to understand and explain the world (Batterman 2001; Chirimuuta 2018; Weber 2022). Accounts with this orientation are guided by scientific methods such as randomized-control trials, gene knock-out experiments, tracer experiments, mathematical reduction techniques, and neural imaging. In addition, these practice-oriented accounts are sensitive to distinct scientific concepts – such as mechanism, pathway, and cascade – and the role these concepts play in untangling unique types of structure and information (Ross In Press). This work is also sensitive to different goals found in explanatory practice and the various types of targets that scientists aim to explain.

Finally, it is important to consider the significance of this topic for discussions in scientific practice, for decisions about what types of research should be supported, and in efforts to improve science communication to various audiences (including the public and experts). Explanation and causality are frequently viewed as foundational topics by researchers working in the life sciences, but there is often significant debate, crosstalk, and differing views on how these should be understood and what it takes for a model or theory to be genuinely explanatory. Even when there is a lack of consensus on this topic in scientific fields, philosophical frameworks can help clarify the distinct positions, assumptions they make, and how they relate to each other, in a way that supports discussion and progress. One way that philosophical frameworks can help is by keeping assessments of the quality of explanations relative to their chosen explanatory target. While distinct scientific explanations can quickly be pitched as rivals, this can be a false comparison if they aim to explain different targets. This can happen when there is interest in explaining different aspects of the same physical system and when the same term is used to refer to the explanatory target, but it is used in different ways throughout the field (such as an interest in explaining "consciousness" or "memory"). Another benefit of philosophical accounts is that they reveal how scientific explanation is often much more of a piecemeal process (in which a system is broken into distinct explanatory targets) as opposed to a complete, full theory or explanation of everything (Woodward 2017). Appreciating these features of explanation as explanandum-relative and piecemeal can help in identifying and assessing candidate explanations in science. Additionally, providing a framework for understanding the logic and structure of scientific explanation matters because it clarifies the standards that should guide which scientific projects are supported and pursued. The specific wording of grant calls and journal guidelines significantly shape which types of scientific work are funded, supported, and valued. When such calls and guidelines emphasize the importance of identifying "mechanisms," or biological causes (over socioenvironmental causes), or reductive approaches to explanation, they can reinforce problematic assumptions about scientific explanation and disincentivize work in important areas of research (such as areas that study environmental, social, and macro-scale causes) (Insel 2022; NIM 2023; Ross and Bassett 2024). Clarifying the standards, logic, and hallmarks of scientific explanation is essential for communicating scientific findings to the public. This arises in efforts to communicate how scientific methods justify their conclusions, what it means to say that a causal mechanism (or pathway, or cascade) has been identified, and what it means to say that we now have a fuller explanation of some phenomenon of interest, whether in biology, neuroscience, medicine, ecology, or some other field.

The analysis provided in this Element provides a picture of scientific explanation in biology and the life sciences that is heterogeneous, complex, and principled. Just as there is no single "scientific method" this work is consistent with their being no single type of "scientific explanation." Of course, there is a balance to strike in capturing the diversity of explanatory patterns in science, while specifying the standards of explanation. Much of the work outlined in this Element aims to capture this nuance, that is, both the variety and limits of scientific explanation.

References

(2023). Support for Clinical Trials at NIMH. www.nimh.nih.gov/funding/opportunities-announcements/clinical-trials-foas.

Adams, C. and Franzosa, R. (2008). *Introduction to topology*. Pearson Prentice Hall, New Delhi.

Andersen, H. (2014a). A Field Guide to Mechanisms: Part I: A Field Guide to Mechanisms I. *Philosophy Compass*, 9(4):274–283.

Andersen, H. (2014b). A Field Guide to Mechanisms: Part II. *Philosophy Compass*, 9(4):284–293.

Andersen, O. S. (2008). Editorial Practices, Scientific Impact, and Scientific Quality. *The Journal of General Physiology*, 131(1):1–3.

Angrist, J. D. and Pischke, J.-S. (2009). *Mostly harmless econometrics: An empiricist's companion*. Princeton University Press, Princeton, NJ.

Ankley, G. T., Bennett, R. S., Erickson, R. J., et al. (2010). Adverse Outcome Pathways: A Conceptual Framework to Support Ecotoxicology Research and Risk Assessment. *Environmental Toxicology and Chemistry*, 29:730–741.

Anscombe, E. (1971). Causality and Determination. In *The collected philosophical papers of G.E.M. Anscombe*, volume 2. Oxford University Press.

Aristotle (1970). *Aristotle's Physics I,II*. Oxford University Press, London.

Baker, A. (2005). Are there Genuine Mathematical Explanations of Physical Phenomena? *Mind*, 114(454):223–238.

Baker, A. (2012). Science-Driven Mathematical Explanation. *Mind*, 121(482):243–267.

Barwich, A.-S. (2021). Imaging the Living Brain: An Argument for Ruthless Reductionism from Olfactory Neurobiology. *Journal of Theoretical Biology*, 512:110560.

Bassett, D. S. and Bullmore, E. T. (2017). Small-World Brain Networks Revisited. *The Neuroscientist*, 23(5):499–516.

Batterman, R. W. (2001). *The devil in the details*. Oxford University Press, Oxford.

Batterman, R. W. (2002). Asymptotics and the Role of Minimal Models. *The British Journal for the Philosophy of Science*, 53(1):21–38.

Batterman, R. W. (2010). On the Explanatory Role of Mathematics in Empirical Science. *The British Journal for the Philosophy of Science*, 61(1):1–25.

Batterman, R. W. (2021). *A middle way: A non-fundamental approach to many-body physics*. Oxford University Press, Oxford, 1st edition.

Batterman, R. W. and Rice, C. C. (2014). Minimal Model Explanations. *Philosophy of Science*, 81(3):349–376.

Bechtel, W. and Richardson, R. C. (2010). *Discovering complexity*. The MIT Press, Cambridge, MA.

Beebee, H. (2004). Causing and Nothingness. In Hall, N. and Paul, L. A., editors, *Causation and counterfactuals*, pages 291–308. The MIT Press, Cambridge, MA.

Bickle, J. (2006). Reducing Mind to Molecular Pathways: Explicating the Reductionism Implicit in Current Cellular and Molecular Neuroscience. *Synthese*, 151(3):411–434.

Bloomfield, M. M. and Stephens, L. J. (1996). *Chemistry and the living organism*, volume 1. John Wiley & Sons, New York.

Bogen, J. and Woodward, J. (1988). Saving the Phenomena. *The Philosophical Review*, 97(3):303.

Boniolo, G. and Campaner, R. (2018). Molecular Pathways and the Contextual Explanation of Molecular Functions. *Biology and Philosophy*, 33(3–4):24.

Brigandt, I. (2010). Beyond Reduction and Pluralism: Toward an Epistemology of Explanatory Integration in Biology. *Erkenntnis*, 73(3):295–311.

Bromberger, S. (1966). Why Questions. In Colodny, R. G., editor, *Mind and cosmos: Essays in contemporary science and philosophy*, pages 86–111. University of Pittsburgh Press, Pittsburgh, PA.

Bromberger, S. (1992). *On what we don't know*. The University of Chicago Press, London.

Butterfield, J. (2011). Emergence, Reduction and Supervenience: A Varied Landscape. *Foundations of Physics*, 41(6):920–959.

Cartwright, N. (1979). Causal Laws and Effective Strategies. *Nous*, 13(4):20.

Cartwright, N. (2004). Causation: One Word, Many Things. *Philosophy of Science*, 71(5):805–819.

Cheng, P. W. (1997). From Covariation to Causation: A Causal Power Theory. *Philosophical Review*, pages 104:1–39.

Chirimuuta, M. (2014). Minimal Models and Canonical Neural Computations: The Distinctness of Computational Explanation in Neuroscience. *Synthese*, 191(2):127–153.

Chirimuuta, M. (2018). Explanation in Computational Neuroscience: Causal and Non-causal. *The British Journal for the Philosophy of Science*, 69(3): 849–880.

Clatterbaugh, K. (1999). *The causation debate in modern philosophy 1637–1739*. Routledge, New York.

Cole, M. W., Ito, T., Bassett, D. S., and Schultz, D. H. (2016). Activity Flow Over Resting-State Networks Shapes Cognitive Task Activations. *Nature Neuroscience*, 19(12):1718–1726.

Craver, C. and Darden, L. (2013). *In search of mechanisms*. The University of Chicago Press, Chicago, IL.

Craver, C. and Tabery, J. (2015). Mechanisms in Science. *Stanford Encyclopedia of Philosophy*.

Craver, C. F. (2007). *Explaining the brain*. Oxford University Press, Oxford.

Davie, E. W. and Ratnoff, O. D. (1964). Waterfall Sequence for Intrinsic Blood Clotting. *Science*, 145:1310–1312.

Dodge, K. A., Malone, P. S., Lansford, J. E., et al. (2009). *A dynamic cascade model of the development of substance-use onset*. Wiley-Blackwell, Oxford.

Dowe, P. (2018). Causal Process. *Stanford Encyclopedia of Philosophy*.

Dupré, J. (2013). Living Causes. *Aristotelian Society Supplementary Volume*, 87(1):19–37.

Endow, S. A. (2003). Kinesin Motors as Molecular Machines. *BioEssays*, 25(12):1212–1219.

Euler, L. (1956). *The seven bridges of Königsberg*, volume 1. Simon and Schuster.

Fodor, J. A. (1974). Special Sciences (Or: The Disunity of Science as a Working Hypothesis). *Synthese*, 28:97–115.

Fornito, A., Zalesky, A., and Bullmore, E. (2016). *Fundamentals of brain network analysis*. Academic Press, San Diego, CA.

Friedman, M. (1974). Explanation and Scientific Understanding. *The Journal of Philosophy*, 71(1):5–19.

Garfinkel, A. (1981). *Forms of explanation*. Yale University. New Haven, CT.

Glennan, S. (2017). *The new mechanical philosophy*. Oxford University Press, Oxford.

Godfrey-Smith, P. (2013). Causal Pluralism. In Beebee, H., Hitchcock, C., and Menzies, P., editors, *The oxford handbook of causation*, 2010, pages 326–337. Oxford University Press, Oxford.

Goldenfeld, N. (1992). *Lectures on phase transitions and the renormalization group*. Springer-Verlag, New York.

Gopnik, A. (2021). Back Cover. In *Causation with a human face*. Oxford University Press, Oxford.

Green, S. and Batterman, R. (2017). Biology Meets Physics: Reductionism and Multi-scale Modeling of Morphogenesis. *Studies in History and Philosophy of Science Part C: Studies in History and Philosophy of Biological and Biomedical Sciences*, 61:20–34.

Griffiths, T. L. and Tenenbaum, J. B. (2005). Structure and Strength in Causal Induction. *Cognitive Psychology*, 51(4):334–384.

Halina, M. (2018). Mechanistic explanation and its limits. Routledge Taylor & Francis Group, New York.

Hempel, C. (1962). Deductive-Nomological vs. Statistical Explanation. In Peigel, H. and Maxwell, G., editors, *Minnesota studies in the philosophy of science*, volume III, pages 98–169. University of Minnesota Press, Minneapolis.

Hempel, C. (1965). *Aspects of scientific explanation*. The Free Press, New York.

Hempel, C. (1991). Laws and Their Role in Scientific Explanation. In Boyd, R., Gasper, P., and Trout, J. D., editors, *The philosophy of science*, pages 299–316. The MIT Press, Cambridge, MA.

Hempel, C. G. and Oppenheim, P. (1948). Studies in the Logic of Explanation. *Philosophy of Science*, 15(2):135–175.

Henry, J. (2001). *The scientific revolution and the origins of modern science*. Studies in European History. Palgrave, New York, 2nd edition.

Hitchcock, C. (2007). How to Be a Causal Pluralist. In Machamer, P. and. Wolters, G., editors, *Thinking about causes*, pages 200–221. University of Pittsburgh Press, Pittsburgh, PA.

Hitchcock, C. (2018). Probabilistic Causation. *Stanford Encyclopedia of Philosophy*.

Hodgkin, A. (1948). The Local Electric Changes Associated with Repetitive Action in Non-medullated Axon. *Journal of Physiology*, 107(2): 165–181.

Hoppensteadt, F. and Izhikevich, E. (1997). *Weakly connected neural networks*. Springer, New York.

Hume, D. (1985). *A treatise of human nature*. Penguin Classics, London.

Huneman, P. (2010). Topological Explanations and Robustness in Biological Sciences. *Synthese*, 177(2):213–245.

Hutchinson, T. (2007). *Intelligent testing strategies in ecotoxicology: Mode of action approach for specifically acting chemicals*. European Centre for Ecotoxicology and Toxicology of Chemicals, Brussels.

Hüttemann, A. and Love, A. (2011). Aspects of Reductive Explanation in Biological Science: Intrinsicality, Fundamentality, and Temporality. *The British Journal for the Philosophy of Science*, 62(3):519–549.

Insel, T. (2022). *Healing: Our path from mental illness to mental health*. Penguin Press, New York.

Ismael, J. (2021). Back Cover. In *Causation with a human face*. Oxford University Press, Oxford.

JAMA (2023). Journal of the American Medical Association (JAMA). https://jamanetwork.com/journals/jama/pages/instructions-for-authors.

Jansson, L. and Saatsi, J. (2017). Explanatory Abstractions. *The British Journal for the Philosophy of Science*, 70(3):817–844.

Kadanoff, L. P. (1990). Scaling and Universality in Statistical Physics. *Physica A: Statistical Mechanics and Its Applications*, 163(1):1–14.

Kaiser, M. (2015). *Reduction explanation in the biological sciences*, volume 16. Springer, London.

Kaplan, D. M. (2017). *Explanation and integration in mind and brain science*. Oxford University Press, Oxford.

Kaplan, D. M. and Craver, C. F. (2011). The Explanatory Force of Dynamical and Mathematical Models in Neuroscience: A Mechanistic Perspective. *Philosophy of Science*, 78(4):601–627.

Karuza, E. A., Thompson-Schill, S. L., and Bassett, D. S. (2016). Local Patterns to Global Architectures: Influences of Network Topology on Human Learning. *Trends in Cognitive Sciences*, 20(8):629–640.

Kendler, K. S. (2005). "A Gene for...": The Nature of Gene Action in Psychiatric Disorders. *American Journal of Psychiatry*, 162(7):1243–1252.

Kitano, H. and Oda, K. (2006). Robustness Trade-Offs and Host–Microbial Symbiosis in the Immune System. *Molecular Systems Biology*, 2:787.

Kitcher, P. (1989). *Explanatory unification and the causal structure of the world*, volume 13. University of Minnesota Press, Minneapolis, MN.

Lange, M. (2013). What Makes a Scientific Explanation Distinctively Mathematical? *The British Journal for the Philosophy of Science*, 64(3):485–511.

Lange, M. (2018). *Because without cause: Non-causal explanations in science and mathematics*. Oxford University Press, Oxford.

Levy, A. and Bechtel, W. (2013). Abstraction and the Organization of Mechanisms. *Philosophy of Science*, 80(2):241–261.

Lewis, D. A. (1986). *Philosophical papers*, volume II. Oxford University Press, Oxford.

Lombrozo, T. (2010). Causal-Explanatory Pluralism: How Intentions, Functions, and Mechanisms Influence Causal Ascriptions. *Cognitive Psychology*, 61(4):303–332.

Ly, C. H., Lynch, G. S., and Ryall, J. G. (2020). A Metabolic Roadmap for Somatic Stem Cell Fate. *Cell Metabolism*, 31(6):1052–1067.

Lyon, A. (2012). Mathematical Explanations of Empirical Facts, and Mathematical Realism. *Australasian Journal of Philosophy*, 90(3):559–578.

Lyon, A. and Colyvan, M. (2008). The Explanatory Power of Phase Spaces. *Philosophia Mathematica*, 16(2):227–243.

Macfarlane, R. G. (1966). The Basis of the Cascade Hypothesis of Blood Clotting. *Thrombosis et Diathesis Haemorrhagica*, 15(03/04):591–602.

Machamer, P., Darden, L., and Craver, C. F. (2000). Thinking about Mechanisms. *Philosophy of Science*, 67:1–25.

Mackie, J. L. (1965). Causes and Conditions. *American Philosophical Quarterly*, 2:245–264.

Maddy, P. (1992). Indispensability and Practice. *The Journal of Philosophy*, 89(6):275.

Mahadevan, L. and Matsudaira, P. (2000). Motility Powered by Supramolecular Springs and Ratchets. *Science*, 288(5463):95–99.

Marina, T. I., Salinas, V., Cordone, G., et al. (2018). The Food Web of Potter Cove (Antarctica): Complexity, Structure and Function. *Estuarine, Coastal and Shelf Science*, 200:141–151.

Masse, N. Y., Yang, G. R., Song, H. F., Wang, X.-J., and Freedman, D. J. (2019). Circuit Mechanisms for the Maintenance and Manipulation of Information in Working Memory. *Nature Neuroscience*, 22(7):1159–1167.

Masten, A. S. and Cicchetti, D. (2010). Developmental Cascades. *Development and Psychopathology*, 22(3):491–495.

Mayr, E. (1989). *Toward a new philosophy of biology: Observations of an evolutionist*. Harvard University Press, Boston, MA.

Mill, J. S. (1874). *A system of logic*. Harper & Brothers, New York, 8th edition.

Mitchell, S. D. (2009). *Unsimple truths*. The University of Chicago Press, Chicago, IL.

Montoya, J. M. and Solé, R. V. (2002). Small World Patterns in Food Webs. *Journal of Theoretical Biology*, 214(3):405–412.

Morris, W. and Brown, C. (2019). David Hume. *Stanford Encyclopedia of Philosophy*.

Nagel, E. (1961). *The structure of science*. Harcout, Brace and World, New York.

O'Malley, M. A., Brigandt, I., Love, A. C., et al. (2014). Multilevel Research Strategies and Biological Systems. *Philosophy of Science*, 81(5):811–828.

Parascandola, M. and Weed, D. L. (2001). Causation in Epidemiology. *Journal of Epidemiology and Community Health*, 55(12):905–912.

Pickrell, J. K., Marioni, J. C., Pai, A. A., et al. (2010). Understanding Mechanisms Underlying Human Gene Expression Variation with RNA Sequencing. *Nature*, 464(7289):768–772.

Pincock, C. (2012). *Mathematics and scientific representation*. Oxford University Press, Oxford.

Potochnik, A. (2007). Optimality Modeling and Explanatory Generality. *Philosophy of Science*, 74(5):680–691.

Potochnik, A. (2021). Our World Isn't Organized into Levels. In Brooks, D. S., DiFrisco, J., Wimsatt, W. C., editors, *Levels of organization in biology*, pages 61–76. MIT Press, Cambridge, MA.

Putnam, H. (1967). Psychological Predicates. In Capitan, W. H. and Merrill, D. D., editors, *Art, mind, and religion*, pages 37–48. University of Pittsburgh Press, Pittsburgh, PA

Reichenbach, H. (1971). *The direction of time*. University of California Press, Berkeley.

Reiss, J. (2009). Causation in the Social Sciences: Evidence, Inference, and Purpose. *Philosophy of the Social Sciences*, 39(1):20–40.

Reutlinger, A. (2016). Is There a Monist Theory of Causal and Noncausal Explanations? The Counterfactual Theory of Scientific Explanation. *Philosophy of Science*, 83:733–745.

Rheinberger, H.-J. (1997). *Toward a history of epistmic things: Synthesizing proteins in the test tube*. Stanford University Press, Stanford, CA.

Rice, C. (2015). Moving Beyond Causes: Optimality Models and Scientific Explanation: Moving Beyond Causes. *Noûs*, 49(3):589–615.

Richardson, L. F. (1922). *Weather prediction by numerical process*. Cambridge University Press, Cambridge.

Ripple, W. J., Estes, J. A., Schmitz, O. J., et al. (2016). What Is a Trophic Cascade? *Trends in Ecology & Evolution*, 31:842–849.

Ross, L. (In Press). Cascade versus Mechanism: The Diversity of Causal Structure in Science. *The British Journal for the Philosophy of Science*.

Ross, L. (2023b). Causal Constraints in the Life and Social Sciences. *Philosophy of Science*, https://doi.org/10.1017/psa.2023.165.

Ross, L. (2023c). The Explanatory Nature of Constraints: Law-Based, Mathematical, and Causal. *Synthese*, 202, 56. https://doi.org/10.1007/s11229-023-04281-5.

Ross, L. (2024). What Is Social Structural Explanation? A Causal Account. *Nous*, 58(1):163–179. https://doi.org/10.1111/nous.12446.

Ross, L. and Woodward, J. (2022). Irreversible (One-Hit) and Reversible (Sustaining) Causation (Forthcoming). *Philosophy of Science*, 89(5):889–898.

Ross, L. N. (2015). Dynamical Models and Explanation in Neuroscience. *Philosophy of Science*, 82(1):32–54.

Ross, L. N. (2018). Causal Selection and the Pathway Concept. *Philosophy of Science*, 85:551–572.

Ross, L. N. (2021). Distinguishing Topological and Causal Explanation. *Synthese*, 198:9803–9820. https://doi.org/10.1007/s11229-020-02685-1.

Ross, L. N. (2020). Multiple Realizability from a Causal Perspective. *Philosophy of Science*, 640–662.

Ross, L. N. (2021a). Causal Concepts in Biology: How Pathways Differ from Mechanisms and Why It Matters. *The British Journal for the Philosophy of Science*, 72:131–158; https://doi.org/10.1093/bjps/axy078.

Ross, L. N. (2021b). Tracers in Neuroscience: Causation, Constraints, and Connectivity. *Synthese*, 199:4077–4095.

Ross, L. N. (2023a). Causes with Material Continuity. *Biology & Philosophy*, 36(52). (https://doi.org/10.1007/s10539-021-09826-x).

Ross, L. N. (2023b). Explanation in Contexts of Causal Complexity: Lessons from Psychiatric Genetics (Forthcoming). In *From scientific metaphysics to biological practice*. Minnesota studies in the philosophy of science.

Ross, L. N. and Bassett, D. S. (2024). Causation in Neuroscience: Keeping Mechanism Meaningful. *Nature Reviews Neuroscience*, 25(2):81–90.

Roth, P. A. (1988). Narrative Explanations: The Case of History. *History and Theory*, 27(1):1.

Salmon, W. (1977). Statistical Explanation. In Salmon, W., Editor, *Statistical explanation and statistical relevance*, pages 29–87. Pittsburgh University Press, Pittsburgh, PA.

Salmon, W. (1989). *Four decades of scientific explanation*. University of Minnesota Press, Minneapolis, MN.

Salmon, W. C. (1984). *Scientific explanation and the causal structure of the world*, number 5. Princeton University Press, Princeton, NJ.

Salmon, W. C. (1997). Causality and Explanation: A Reply to Two Critiques. *Philosophy of Science*, 64:461–477.

Seals, D. R. (2023). Publishing Particulars: Part 3. General Writing Tips, Editing, and Responding to Peer Review. *American Journal of Physiology-Regulatory, Integrative and Comparative Physiology*, 324(3):R409–R424.

Shadish, W., Cook, T., and Campbell, D. (2002). *Experimental and quasi-experimental designs for generalized causal inference*, volume 100. Houghton Mifflin, Boston, MA.

Silberstein, M. and Chemero, A. (2013). Constraints on Localization and Decomposition as Explanatory Strategies in the Biological Sciences. *Philosophy of Science*, 80(5):958–970.

Skillings, D. J. (2015). Mechanistic Explanation of Biological Processes. *Philosophy of Science*, 82(5):1139–1151.

Skow, B. (2014). Are There Non-causal Explanations (of Particular Events)? *The British Journal for the Philosophy of Science*, 65(3):445–467.

Skyrms, B. (1980). *Causal necessity*. Yale University Press, New Haven, CT.

Smolyak, A., Levy, O., Vodenska, I., Buldyrev, S., and Havlin, S. (2020). Mitigation of Cascading Failures in Complex Networks. *Nature: Scientific Reports* 10:1–12.

Sober, E. (1983). Equilibrium Explanation. *Philosophical Studies*, 43(2): 201–210.

Sober, E. (1999). The Multiple Realizability Argument against Reduction. *Philosophy of Science*, 66:42–564.

Stein, H. F. (1990). *American medicine as culture.* Taylor and Francis, New York.

Strevens, M. (2008). *Depth: An account of scientific explanation.* Harvard University Press, Cambridge, MA.

Suppes, P. (1970). *A probabilistic theory of causality.* North-Holland, Amsterdam.

Taylor, C. M., Wang, Q., Rosa, B. A., et al. (2013). Discovery of Anthelmintic Drug Targets and Drugs Using Chokepoints in Nematode Metabolic Pathways. *PLoS Pathogens*, 9(8):1–17.

Vasilyeva, N., Blanchard, T., and Lombrozo, T. (2018). Stable Causal Relationships Are Better Causal Relationships. *Cognitive Science*, 42(4):1265–1296.

Wakil, S. and Justus, J. (2017). Mathematical Explanation and the Biological Optimality Fallacy. *Philosophy of Science*, 84(5):916–930.

Waters, C. K. (1990). Why the Anti-reductionist Consensus Won't Survive: The Case of Classical Mendelian Genetics. *Philosophy of Science*, 1990:125–139.

Waters, C. K. (2007). Causes that Make a Difference. *The Journal of Philosophy*, 104(11), 1–30.

Waters, C. K. (2009). Beyond Theoretical Reduction and Layer-Cake Antireduction: How DNA Retooled Genetics and Transformed Biological Practice. In Ruse, M., editor, *The Oxford handbook of philosophy of biology*, pages 238–262. Oxford University Press, Oxford, 1st edition.

Watts, D. J. and Strogatz, S. H. (1998). Collective Dynamics of "Small-World" Networks. *Nature*, 393: 440–442.

Weber, M. (2008). Causes without Mechanisms: Experimental Regularities, Physical Laws, and Neuroscientific Explanation. *Philosophy of Science*, 75:995–1007.

Weber, M. (2017). Causal Selection versus Causal Parity in Biology: Relevant Counterfactuals and Biologically Normal Interventions (Forthcoming). In *Causation in biology*. Minnesota studies in the philosophy of science.

Weber, M. (2022). *Philosophy of developmental biology.* Cambridge University Press, Cambridge, 1st edition.

Wilson, M. (2021). *Imitation of rigor.* Oxford University Press, Oxford.

Wimsatt, W. C. (1972). Complexity and Organization. *Philosophy of Science*, 1972:67–86.

Wimsatt, W. C. (1976). Reductionism, Levels of Organization, and the Mind-body Problem. In Globus, G. G., Maxwell, G., and Savodnik, I., editors, *Consciousness and the Brain.* Springer, Boston, MA.

Woodward, J. (2003). *Making things happen*. Oxford University Press, Oxford.

Woodward, J. (2010). Causation in Biology: Stability, Specificity, and the Choice of Levels of Explanation. *Biology & Philosophy*, 25(3):287–318.

Woodward, J. (2013). Mechanistic Explanation: Its Scope and Limits. *Proceedings of the Aristotelian Society*, LXXXVII:39–65.

Woodward, J. (2017). Explanation in Neurobiology: An Interventionist Perspective. In Kaplan, M., Editor, *Explanation and integration in mind and brain science*, pages 70–100. Oxford University Press, Oxford.

Woodward, J. (2019). Some Varieties of Non-causal Explanation. In Reutlinger, A. and Saatsi, J., editors, *Explanation beyond causation: Philosophical perspectives on non-causal explanation*, pages 117–140. Oxford University Press, Oxford.

Woodward, J. (2021). *Causation with a human face*. Oxford University Press, Oxford.

Woodward, J. and Ross, L. (2021). Scientific Explanation. *Stanford Encyclopedia of Philosophy*.

Woodward, J. F. (2016). Causation and Manipulability. *Stanford Encyclopedia of Philosophy*.

Wright, L. (1973). Functions. *The Philosophical Review*, 82(2):139–168.

Wright, L. (1976). *Teleological explanations: An etiological analysis of goals and functions*. University of California Press, London.

Zheng, S., Tan, W., Li, X., et al. (2021). Aged Monkeys Fed a High-Fat/High-Sugar Diet Recapitulate Metabolic Disorders and Cardiac Contractile Dysfunction. *Journal of Cardiovascular Translational Research*, 14(5):799–815.

Zöller, D., Sandini, C., Schaer, M., et al. (2021). Structural Control Energy of Resting-State Functional Brain States Reveals Less Cost-Effective Brain Dynamics in Psychosis Vulnerability. *Human Brain Mapping*, 42(7):2181–2200.

Acknowledgements

I would like to thank Jim Woodward, Ken Kendler, Bob Batterman and two anonymous reviewers for their helpful comments on this Element. Additionally, I would like to thank Jim Woodward for his mentorship, support, friendship, and contributions to philosophy and science. His research has served as a reliable guide – to me and many others – in thinking about causation and explanation. Funding for this project was provided by a National Science Foundation (NSF) Career Award (#1945647) and a John Templeton Foundation Grant Award (#63021). There are many others that I would like to acknowledge for their support, including: Gregory Ross, Sherry Mueller, Jacqueline Leopold, Leah Anderson, Rosalyn Laudati, Danielle Thomsen, and Megan Delehanty.

This book is dedicated to my dad, mom, and sister for everything.

Cambridge Elements ☰

Philosophy of Biology

Grant Ramsey
KU Leuven

Grant Ramsey is a BOFZAP research professor at the Institute of Philosophy, KU Leuven, Belgium. His work centers on philosophical problems at the foundation of evolutionary biology. He has been awarded the Popper Prize twice for his work in this area. He also publishes in the philosophy of animal behavior, human nature and the moral emotions. He runs the Ramsey Lab (theramseylab.org), a highly collaborative research group focused on issues in the philosophy of the life sciences.

Michael Ruse
Florida State University

Michael Ruse is the Lucyle T. Werkmeister Professor of Philosophy and the Director of the Program in the History and Philosophy of Science at Florida State University. He is Professor Emeritus at the University of Guelph, in Ontario, Canada. He is a former Guggenheim fellow and Gifford lecturer. He is the author or editor of over sixty books, most recently *Darwinism as Religion: What Literature Tells Us about Evolution*; *On Purpose*; *The Problem of War: Darwinism, Christianity, and their Battle to Understand Human Conflict*; and *A Meaning to Life*.

About the Series

This Cambridge Elements series provides concise and structured introductions to all of the central topics in the philosophy of biology. Contributors to the series are cutting-edge researchers who offer balanced, comprehensive coverage of multiple perspectives, while also developing new ideas and arguments from a unique viewpoint.

Cambridge Elements ≡

Philosophy of Biology

Printed in the United States
by Baker & Taylor Publisher Services